22 Comedy Ten-Minute Plays

Royalty-free Plays for Teens and Young Adults

Laurie Allen

MERIWETHER PUBLISHING
A division of Pioneer Drama Service, Inc.
Denver, Colorado

Meriwether Publishing
A division of Pioneer Drama Service, Inc.
PO Box 4267
Englewood, CO 80155-4267

www.pioneerdrama.com

Printed in the United States of America
First Edition

Library of Congress Cataloging-in-Publication Data

Names: Allen, Laurie, 1962- author.
Title: 22 comedy ten-minute plays : scenes for teens and young adults / by Laurie Allen.
Other titles: Twenty-two comedy ten-minute plays
Description: First edition. | Englewood, CO : Meriwether Publishing, a division of Pioneer Drama Service, Inc., [2019] | Audience: Ages: 13 to 18. | Audience: Grades: 9 to 12.
Identifiers: LCCN 2019001465 | ISBN 9781566082112 (pbk. : alk. paper)
Subjects: LCSH: Young adult drama, American.
Classification: LCC PS3601.L4324 A19 2019 | DDC 812/.6--dc23

LC record available at https://lccn.loc.gov/2019001465

2   3   4   20   21   22

CONTENTS

THE NEW METEOROLOGIST (5E) 1

POP QUIZ (2F, 4E) 10

GUARDIAN ANGEL (1M, 1E) 17

LOVE AT FIRST SIGHT (2M, 4F, plus extras) 24

NO SOLICITORS ALLOWED (1M, 1F) 31

BEST ACTRESS (2F, 2E) 37

FINDERS KEEPERS (2F, 6E) 43

GENESIS (1M, 1F, 2E) 52

JUST A TRIM (1M, 1F) 59

DRIVING LESSON (1M, 1F, 2E) 65

UP CLOSE AND PERSONAL (1F, 2E) 73

JOB FAIR (3M, 2F, 1E) 80

DELAYED (1M, 2F) 88

STRANGE ADDICTIONS (2M, 1F, 1E) 94

FREE ADVICE (2M, 2F, 1E) 102

HOMECOMING QUEEN (3M, 2F) 109

WEDDING PLANS (2M, 2F) 114

THE DEATH OF ANTS (1M, 1F) 123

THE EYE EXAM (1M, 3E) 130

PHONE-FREE ZONE (2E, plus at least 12 extras) 137

THE FORT (4F) 143

FOREVER HAS NOW ARRIVED (1M, 1F, 1E) 148

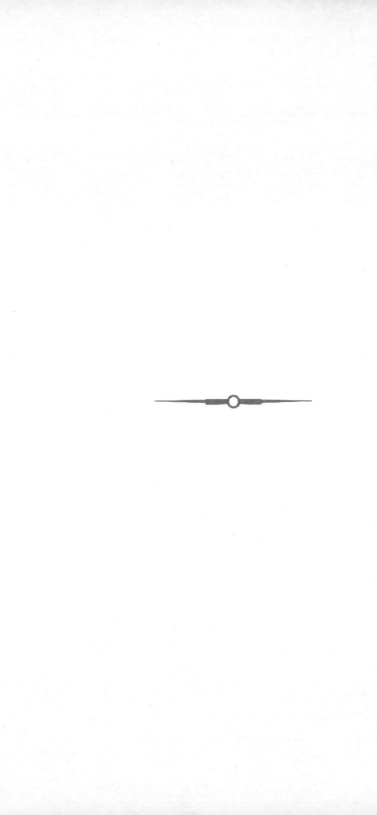

THE NEW METEOROLOGIST

CAST OF CHARACTERS

PRODUCER (E)................................ head of the news station
NEWS ANCHOR (E) ....prima donna
SPORTSCASTER (E)...pizza fan
MAKEUP ARTIST (E) ....head stylist
EMILY (E).. pizza delivery person

SETTING
A news station.

PROPERTIES
News desk, chairs. Three cell phones, headset, notes, makeup powder and brush, thick packet of papers, breath spray, pizza box, cash, seasoning packets, monitor, jacket, camera.

LIGHTS UP on PRODUCER, wearing a headset, talking on her cell phone, and pacing back and forth. NEWS ANCHOR and SPORTSCASTER are sitting behind a news desk, prepping for the news to begin in a few minutes. NEWS ANCHOR reviews his notes while SPORTSCASTER checks game scores on her phone. MAKEUP ARTIST puts on their final touches then EXITS.

PRODUCER: *(Into her phone.)* What do you mean you're sick? *(Listens.)* What? It just came on suddenly? Well, what am I supposed to do? We go live in a few minutes, and I'm down a meteorologist?! *(Listens.)* So, what am I supposed to do? Show pictures of the upcoming conditions with no reporter in sight and let them guess the weather forecast?! *(Hangs up and screams, then rushes to NEWS ANCHOR.)* Listen here—

NEWS ANCHOR: Oh, no! Don't even ask. I don't do weather. I only do top stories and occasionally breaking news. Breaking news is the best. Gets the heart pumping and the adrenaline going. *(As if live.)* This just in! Police have

1

confirmed that the stolen cemetery flowers were taken by a
florist who was hoping to increase sales!

PRODUCER: Oh, come on! Just this once? I'm in a bind!

NEWS ANCHOR: Look, I only do cold hard facts. Not
predictions.

PRODUCER: What's wrong with predictions?

NEWS ANCHOR: What's wrong with them? I'll tell you what's
wrong. Our audience gets mad when our weather prediction
turns out to be wrong. And around here, it's often wrong!
I don't need the stress. I'll just stick to the cold hard facts,
thank you very much!

PRODUCER: *(Turns to SPORTSCASTER.)* You can't
stop thinking sports for a second, can you? Stop looking
at the scores!

SPORTSCASTER: But the Yankees won yesterday.

PRODUCER: I don't care. It's up to you!

SPORTSCASTER: Oh, no. My contract clearly states that
I only do sports. Sports. That's it. You'll have to find
someone else.

PRODUCER: I don't remember seeing that in your contract.

SPORTSCASTER: *(Pulls out a thick contract and quickly flips
through several pages before pointing.)* Right here. Clause
sixteen point two. Right under appearance at community
events must be made at least six weeks prior to the date of
the event. See? Sportscaster is strictly limited to covering the
sports and is not required to sub for anchors, reporters, or
meteorologists. So… *(Puts the contract away.)*

PRODUCER: Please! Just this once?

SPORTSCASTER: Contact my agent if you have any questions.
Sorry. The only time I have to talk about weather is if a
game is rained out. Other than that, I don't do weather.

PRODUCER: *(Turns back to NEWS ANCHOR and slams
her hands on the desk.)* Come on! Can't you fill in? Just
this once?

NEWS ANCHOR: Forget it. I'm a respected news anchor with
nail-biting, eye-opening, life-changing reports. Not little
guesses about whether it's going to be windy or cloudy.
Sorry. *(Clears his throat, sprays breath freshener, and warms
up his voice.)* Hummm…

PRODUCER: Well, I've got to find someone! And fast! *(Dials her phone. EMILY ENTERS holding a pizza box. She stops and waits for someone to notice her.)*

NEWS ANCHOR: *(Practices.)* Good evening, from Channel One News. *(Sprays freshener in his mouth again, then continues various vocal and physical warm-ups.)* Good evening. Good evening. Good evening. Good evening, from Channel One News.

SPORTSCASTER: *(Rehearses.)* The Mets have done it again! Lost. Will they continue with their losing streak or surprise us and actually win a game?

NEWS ANCHOR: No surprises. They're terrible this year.

SPORTSCASTER: I know, but we must keep the audience in suspense.

PRODUCER: *(Notices EMILY.)* What are you doing in here? We're about to start the newscast.

EMILY: Uh… someone ordered a pepperoni pizza.

SPORTSCASTER: *(Raises her hand.)* Hey! Over here! That was me. *(Takes cash from her pocket as EMILY places the pizza on the desk.)* There's enough here for a tip.

EMILY: Thank you. Do you need any parmesan or red pepper?

SPORTSCASTER: Oh, I sure do! *(EMILY digs in her pocket and pulls out a packet of each.)*

PRODUCER: You can't eat that now!

NEWS ANCHOR: Oooh! Can I have a piece?

SPORTSCASTER: Sure!

PRODUCER: Did you hear me? We're about to go on live!

SPORTSCASTER: *(Puts the box under the desk.)* I'll eat it during the commercials then. *(To EMILY.)* Hey, what's it like outside? I don't want the Yankees game rained out again.

EMILY: Oh, it's not bad. It's partly cloudy and about seventy degrees. *(Starts to leave.)*

PRODUCER: *(To EMILY.)* Stop! Wait right there!

EMILY: *(Stops and turns.)* Were you talking to me?

PRODUCER: Yeah! What did you say about the weather?

EMILY: That it's partly cloudy. And around seventy outside.

PRODUCER: *(Rushes to her.)* Can you read? Say, read off a monitor? *(Points.)* Like that monitor over there by the camera?

EMILY: Of course I can read.

PRODUCER: Let me hear you. Try it.

EMILY: Okay. *(Looks at the monitor.)* "After a wet start, rain will clear eastward followed by much drier weather for the second half of the night."

PRODUCER: Perfect! You're hired!

EMILY: Hired? To do what?

PRODUCER: *(Wildly shakes her hand.)* Congratulations! You're our new meteorologist tonight!

EMILY: I am?

PRODUCER: You are!

EMILY: Wow! Just like that?

PRODUCER: Just like that.

EMILY: I'm glad you were my last delivery for the day! When do I start?

PRODUCER: *(Looks at her phone.)* In two minutes. *(Leads her to her spot.)* So, just stand right here and read the monitor when the red light comes on. See. That's all there is to it. Never mind the green screen behind you. You won't see the maps anyway, but we'll show them to our audience. So, all you have to do is read. Clearly and slowly just like you showed me you could do a minute ago. *(Hollers.)* Can we get makeup over here?

MAKEUP ARTIST: *(Rushes IN with makeup powder and a brush.)* What's the problem?

PRODUCER: Fix her! She goes on in two minutes.

MAKEUP ARTIST: I can't do miracles here. This would take hours.

PRODUCER: Well, just do what you can!

MAKEUP ARTIST: Okay. *(Quickly applies makeup.)*

PRODUCER: She needs a jacket! Can someone find me a jacket for the new meteorologist? *(Rushes OFF.)*

MAKEUP ARTIST: Congrats on the new job.

EMILY: Thanks. It was just so fast. I mean, one minute I'm delivering pizzas and the next I'm the new meatier-ologist. Get it? Meatier…

MAKEUP ARTIST: *(Pause.)* Sure. You know, they don't last long around here.

EMILY: Why not?

MAKEUP ARTIST: The producer is very demanding. She can wear you down rather fast, so just relax, take a deep breath, and you'll do fine. And if she starts screaming at you, basically just ignore her and do what your gut tells you to do.

EMILY: Do what my gut says?

MAKEUP ARTIST: Exactly. She can't fire you. Believe me, she needs you.

EMILY: Thanks for the advice.

MAKEUP ARTIST: Anytime. Welcome aboard. *(Does a few more things to her face and hair.)*

EMILY: I should call my mom. Tell her to watch the news tonight. She'll be surprised to see me on it.

MAKEUP ARTIST: You don't have much time. You go on first. Our viewers like a sneak peek of the weather at the top of the news.

PRODUCER: *(Rushes IN, carrying a jacket.)* Here! Put this on! *(Helps EMILY put on the jacket.)* Perfect! What a transformation. Now, listen, it's really simple. All you need to do is read the monitor. We put up the appropriate weather pictures next to you. So just do this. *(Gently holds out her hand.)* "Today's highs will reach seventy-two degrees." See. Isn't that simple?

EMILY: Yes. I can do that.

PRODUCER: Great! And don't forget to smile. *(Jumps back.)* Okay, people, we're on in five, four, three… *(Uses her fingers for the two and one.)*

EMILY: *(Nervously smiles at the camera.)* Hi. I'm Emily, your new meteorologist, and I'm here to deliver… uh, not pizza… but deliver your forecast. Tonight, increasing clouds with a low around fifty. *(Suddenly remembers to hold her hand and point to the green screen.)*

PRODUCER: *(Loud whisper.)* Other side! Point to the other side!

EMILY: *(Quickly switches arms and points the other direction.)* Tonight, increasing clouds with a low around fifty. Breezy, with a south-southwest wind between fifteen and twenty miles per hour. *(Smiles.)* Which means, it'll be a bit chilly tonight, so don't forget your jackets out there!

PRODUCER: *(Loud whisper.)* That's not on the monitor! Just read what's on the monitor!

EMILY: *(Suddenly freezes as she realizes she's on TV. After a moment, she gives a big smile.)* Wow. I'm on live TV. This is crazy. *(A big wave.)* Hi, Mom! Hope you're watching!

PRODUCER: Just read the monitor! Oh, my gosh! *(Paces.)* This will be the end of me!

EMILY: And here's a small slice of your five-day forecast... *(Holds out the wrong hand again.)*

PRODUCER: Other side! Other side!

EMILY: Sorry. That was just a fly headed to the news desk in hopes of getting a little bite of pepperoni pizza. Can we say "yum"? Thin and crispy is my favorite, what about you? *(Switches arms.)* Now, here's a small slice of your five-day forecast. Which I wouldn't trust all that much because, honestly, how many times do we get it right? We say zero percent chance of rain, you leave your umbrella at home and get soaked.

PRODUCER: What are you doing?

SPORTSCASTER: Told you, you can't trust forecasters!

EMILY: We say eighty percent chance of rain, and you never see a cloud in the sky but you're toting around your umbrella like a complete idiot. So, what's my take on all this?

PRODUCER: We don't want to know! Just read the monitor!

NEWS ANCHOR: I kind of want to see where she's going with this.

EMILY: Life's too short to get all uptight over a little thing like the weather. If it's hot, well, thank goodness it's not cold! And if it's cold, well, thank goodness it's not hot. You know what I mean? Life's like pizza—it's good either way!

PRODUCER: *(Pulls her hair out.)* Where is she getting all of this?

EMILY: It may be a bit cheesy, but it's true.

PRODUCER: *(Into her headphones.)* Can we go to a commercial break? Why not? Well, I need a commercial break now!

SPORTSCASTER: I need some of this pizza now...

EMILY: So, does the weather forecast really matter? Let's spend a little less time worrying and a little more time thinking about our own pie-in-the-sky dreams.

PRODUCER: *(Wildly waves and points to NEWS ANCHOR.)* Jump in! Jump in!

NEWS ANCHOR: *(Clears his throat and looks ahead.)* Now to the nightly news…

EMILY: Hold on. I'm not finished.

PRODUCER: *(Into her headphones.)* How about a break now? Why not? *(To NEWS ANCHOR.)* Go! Go!

NEWS ANCHOR: Topping our stories tonight, two donut thieves were caught in a high school parking lot after getting away with five dozen jelly donuts.

EMILY: Cloudy with a chance of donuts! *(To NEWS ANCHOR.)* Really? That's such old news. Hardly breaking news. It was all over social media this morning. *(To the camera.)* So, let me give you the scoop.

NEWS ANCHOR: Excuse me! This is my breaking story!

SPORTSCASTER: Can we move on to the sports? I have some final scores to announce.

EMILY: The donut thieves said it was part of an elaborate prank. The thieves, high school students, removed the jelly filling and replaced it with mustard. Why mustard donuts, you might ask? Outgoing seniors are known to give incoming freshman a little, shall we say, welcoming. "It's all in good fun," the seniors say. *(Smiles.)* Good, clean fun, so let's not make more of it than that.

NEWS ANCHOR: You're stealing my story! In other breaking news—

SPORTSCASTER: If I may, we have breaking news in the sports world.

EMILY: *(Holds out her phone.)* And let me add this. If you will download this weather app, you'll never have to watch TV again to get your local weather. Right here. Accurate forecast at your fingertips. My generation, well, we don't watch TV for weather updates or news. I mean, forget it. *(Holds up her phone.)* This is how we get our news.

PRODUCER: *(Into headset.)* We need to break to a commercial now! I said now! *(Beat.)* Finally! We've gone to a commercial. *(To OTHERS.)* What is it with you people?! *(Points to EMILY.)* And you… you…!

SPORTSCASTER: Well, if we aren't getting to the sports… *(Flops the pizza box on the desk.)* …I'm eating my pizza! *(Pulls out her phone.)* And checking out the Kentucky Derby.

NEWS ANCHOR: Oh, can I have a piece?

PRODUCER: *(Snaps her fingers at SPORTSCASTER.)* No eating pizza during the broadcast! And put away your phone! You're about to go on with breaking news!

NEWS ANCHOR: Not sure I have any. *(To SPORTSCASTER.)* What was the breaking news in the sports world?

SPORTSCASTER: Oh, somebody beat somebody in tennis. Record setting scores, I think.

NEWS ANCHOR: Eh, not really my favorite sport.

SPORTSCASTER: Mine neither. In fact, I don't watch a lot of sports. It's just this job came up, and, well, I needed it to pay rent. Before this, I actually worked at a pizza place.

NEWS ANCHOR: And you didn't get sick of eating it?

SPORTSCASTER: Who gets sick of eating pizza?

MAKEUP ARTIST: *(Rushes IN.)* The phones are ringing off the hook, and the comments on our Facebook page are coming in by the hundreds!

PRODUCER: Oh, I'm sure they are!

MAKEUP ARTIST: Everyone loves the new meteorologist!

PRODUCER: What?!

EMILY: They do?

MAKEUP ARTIST: They say she's the freshest and best thing that's happened to our station in a long time, and they'll be watching from now on!

PRODUCER: What? I can't believe this!

NEWS ANCHOR: She's okay, I guess.

SPORTSCASTER: A fresh face around here isn't so bad. Liven things up a bit.

EMILY: They like me?

MAKEUP ARTIST: They love you!

EMILY: Wow. I guess I stole a "pizza" their hearts! *(ALL groan.)* Well, thanks for this opportunity, but I'd better get moving. *(Starts to leave.)*

PRODUCER: Wait! Where are you going?

EMILY: My shift is over, so I was headed home after this.

PRODUCER: Oh, no you don't! We're back on in less than one minute, and I need you back in your spot.

EMILY: Are you sure?

PRODUCER: I'm sure. Now get over there and do your stuff. We're on in five, four, three… *(Hand motions two and one.)*

EMILY: Hi, I'm Emily, your new meteorologist.

PRODUCER: *(Sits on the news desk, talks to NEWS ANCHOR and SPORTSCASTER.)* Maybe it is time to celebrate. If she's a hit, then I'm a hit. So, I'm thinking pizza party. Can I have a piece? *(LIGHTS FADE to BLACK.)*

POP QUIZ

CAST OF CHARACTERS

MRS. MOORE (E)...history teacher
ETHAN (E)...student
LAUREN (F)..another
JUSTIN (E)..another
ALEXIS (F)..another
LUIS (E)...another

SETTING
A high school classroom.

PROPERTIES
Five student desks with chairs. Watch, folder, textbooks, papers, bag of chips, backpacks, phones, makeup case with compact inside, water bottle, pencils.

LIGHTS UP on MRS. MOORE, standing in front of her classroom. ETHAN, LAUREN, JUSTIN, ALEXIS, and LUIS sit at their desks. MRS. MOORE looks at her watch and picks up a folder.

MRS. MOORE: I have a student report that I need to hand deliver to our principal. I need to speak briefly to him as well. Relax. It's not about any of you. I won't be long. Ethan, would you mind taking over the class for me while I'm gone?

ETHAN: Who? Me?

MRS. MOORE: Yes, you. Do you mind?

ETHAN: Uh… okay. Sure. *(Stands and goes to the front of the room.)*

MRS. MOORE: *(Points to a textbook.)* You can review our studies from yesterday. Here are my notes. Or if you'd rather not do that, just have the class read the next chapter.

Chapter eighteen. Or here's a word search that you can hand out. Or… give it a shot at teaching. I trust you, Ethan.

ETHAN: Really? I can do what I want?

MRS. MOORE: Yes. Review, read, hand out the word search, whatever you feel compelled to do. And thank you. I won't be long. *(EXITS.)*

ETHAN: *(Clears his throat, nervous, but as he looks around, he suddenly feels a sense of power and authority.)* Pop quiz! *(ALL moan.)*

LAUREN: You can't do that!

JUSTIN: Yeah! You're not the teacher.

ALEXIS: Nice try, Ethan. *(Takes out her phone.)* I have some text messages to respond to.

LUIS: Nap time for me. *(Puts his head on his desk.)*

JUSTIN: Snack time for me. *(Pulls chips from his backpack.)*

LAUREN: I need to check my makeup. *(Grabs her makeup case and examines herself in a compact.)* Hopefully this meeting takes longer than Mrs. Moore expects.

JUSTIN: Yeah, like the rest of the period.

ETHAN: *(Authoritative.)* This will count as a grade!

LUIS: *(Lifts his head and looks around.)* Is anyone taking this test?

LAUREN: Hey, Alexis, can I French braid your hair?

ALEXIS: Sure! I haven't learned how to do that yet. Maybe you can teach me sometime?

LAUREN: Sure! *(Crosses behind ALEXIS and gathers her hair.)* It'll look cute on you.

ETHAN: *(Clears his throat.)* I said… pop quiz! *(ALL ignore him.)*

JUSTIN: *(Takes out his phone and speaks as he texts.)* Easy breezy. Teach left class, so it's… *(Sing-songs.)* …free time! *(Puts his feet on the desk and continues texting.)* The last excuse that worked for me is my hamster died. Add a few tears and a lip quiver, and you're golden.

LAUREN: *(To ALEXIS.)* What mascara do you use? Your eyelashes are so long and pretty.

JUSTIN: I love these chips! Fire Blazin' Hot! Oooh… I need a drink! My mouth is on fire! But it's a good fire! Hot, hot, hot! *(Takes a water bottle from his backpack and drinks.)*

ALEXIS: It's the new 4D mascara. I love the way it extends my eyelashes. Do you want to try it after you finish my hair?

LAUREN: Yes! I'd love to.

ETHAN: *(Raises his voice.)* I said, pop quiz!

LAUREN: Anyway… did you buy that online?

ALEXIS: I did. *(Pulls out phone.)* Here, let me show you the website.

LAUREN: Nice!

JUSTIN: *(Laughs, then texts.)* Or you could say it was your grandmother—

ETHAN: *(Yells.)* Famous people you should know! Question number one!

LUIS: *(Lifts his head.)* Why is he yelling?

JUSTIN: *(Takes another drink. To ETHAN.)* Dude, take it down a notch. We're all enjoying a break here. You should too.

ETHAN: Who was the nineteenth century American soldier who served and died in the Battle of the Alamo?

LAUREN: *(To ALEXIS.)* I don't know. Do you know?

ALEXIS: I don't remember.

JUSTIN: Seriously, Ethan, do you really expect us to take your pop quiz?

ETHAN: *(Points to ALEXIS.)* Put your phone away, please. *(Points to LAUREN.)* And you need to sit down. *(Claps his hands.)* Luis, wake up. This is not nap time. And Justin, put your phone and the food away too. Lauren, no makeup during class. You can do that after the bell rings. *(ALL ignore him. ETHAN crosses to ALEXIS and holds out his hand.)* Phone, please.

ALEXIS: You can't take my phone. You're not the teacher.

ETHAN: I can. I'm your teacher for the moment, so either you hand it over to me or you put it away.

LUIS: Come on. Who cares? Really? The teacher's not in the room.

ETHAN: *(Points to a corner of the room.)* What's that? Is that a camera?

LAUREN: Uh-oh! *(Rushes back to her chair.)*

JUSTIN: Camera? *(Puts away his food.)*

ALEXIS: It is a camera! *(Puts away her phone and makeup.)*

LUIS: *(Sits up straight.)* What camera? *(ALL point.)* Oh!

ETHAN: Maybe—just maybe—this is Mrs. Moore's way of testing us. You know how she's always talking about how there are no neutral moments. How we are accountable for the good and the bad choices we make.

ALEXIS: Being disrespectful or considerate.

LAUREN: Wasting time or studying.

JUSTIN: What we put in our minds and what comes out of our mouths.

LUIS: Staying up half the night playing video games or getting a good night's rest.

ALL: There are no neutral moments.

ETHAN: Question number one. Again, these are about famous people you should know. *(The OTHERS take out pencils and paper.)* Who was the nineteenth century American soldier who served and died in the Battle of the Alamo? *(They stare blankly at their papers. After a moment, LAUREN raises her hand.)* Yes?

LAUREN: I remember the Battle of the Alamo, but I just can't think of his name. Can you narrow it down for us? Like give us a few names to choose from?

ETHAN: This isn't a multiple-choice test.

ALEXIS: Come on, Ethan. Give us a hint. Please?!

LUIS: Yeah, come on. Please?!

JUSTIN: The name, the name. I just can't remember the name!

ETHAN: All right, all right, all right! But after this one, you're on your own. Here are your choices. Andrew Jackson. Paul Revere. Davy Crockett. Or Sam Houston.

JUSTIN: I'm guessing Andrew Jackson.

LAUREN: No, he was the seventh president. Not him.

ALEXIS: Sam Houston. I think that's it.

LUIS: Yeah, he had something to do with Texas since there's a city named after him, and I know the Battle of the Alamo was in Texas.

LAUREN: Sounds right to me.

JUSTIN: I'll go with that. Sam Houston. *(They write down their answers.)*

ETHAN: Wrong! Davy Crockett is a Texas hero because of his role in the Texas Revolution and the Battle of the Alamo.

JUSTIN: That's the name I was thinking of!

ALEXIS: Oh, yeah! Now I remember!

LAUREN: Me too!

LUIS: Okay, not Sam Houston... *(Changes his answer.)* Davy Crockett. Well, you learn something new every day. *(They all change their answers.)*

LAUREN: How could we have forgotten that?

ALEXIS: Well, we won't forget it now.

ETHAN: Question number two. At the end of the sixteenth century, William Shakespeare joined the company of what London Theatre?

LAUREN: Broadway!

ALEXIS: Good answer, Lauren!

JUSTIN: Sixteenth century? Like the 1500s? Was Broadway around then?

LUIS: No, no! I know this one, people. I'm in theatre. Mr. Long taught us this in drama class.

JUSTIN: Speak up, man.

LUIS: The Globe.

ETHAN: Correct! *(They all nod and write their answers.)* In 1599, Shakespeare became an actor and a playwright in the company of the Globe Theatre.

ALEXIS: We're so smart.

LAUREN: Totally.

ETHAN: Last question.

LUIS: Thank goodness.

ETHAN: Who was the first Western explorer to reach China?

ALEXIS: Uh...

JUSTIN: This one is hard.

LUIS: Didn't learn this one in drama class.

LAUREN: I know this one! *(They all smile, relieved.)*

ETHAN: You may not, I repeat, not speak this answer aloud.

LAUREN: I won't. *(The others moan.)* But I will say this...

LUIS: Tell us!

LAUREN: I love playing this game in the swimming pool. *(The others think.)*

JUSTIN: *(Suddenly.)* Marco Polo! *(ETHAN does a face palm.)*

LUIS: Marco.

ALEXIS: Polo.

LAUREN: Marco.

JUSTIN: Polo.

LAUREN: We're so smart.

LUIS: Totally.

ETHAN: Geez! It's not even worth grading our papers.

ALEXIS: I got one hundred.

LAUREN: Me too.

JUSTIN: Aced this pop quiz. For once in my life.

LUIS: Yeah, I needed this grade, but...

JUSTIN: But?

LUIS: *(Throws his paper in the air.)* It probably won't even count since Mrs. Moore isn't here. *(ALL moan as MRS. MOORE ENTERS.)*

MRS. MOORE: Hello, class. It's so nice to walk in here and see you behaving. And I must admit, that I peeked in on you from the camera... *(Points.)* ...and saw that you were all behaving and actually doing classwork. I'm so impressed!

ETHAN: I gave them a pop quiz, Mrs. Moore. About famous people.

MRS. MOORE: Why, thank you for your leadership, Ethan. I'm very impressed. And how did the pop quiz go?

ETHAN: Excellent. They did remarkably well.

ALEXIS: I got a hundred!

LAUREN: Me too.

LUIS: We all did!

MRS. MOORE: That's wonderful! And because of your good behavior while I was absent, I'm going to accept this grade not once, but twice in the grade book. Even for you, Ethan. *(ALL cheer.)*

LAUREN: *(Raises her hand.)* But, Mrs. Moore...

MRS. MOORE: Yes, Lauren?

LAUREN: Well...

MRS. MOORE: What is it?

LAUREN: Well, we did have some help on the pop quiz.

ALEXIS: Yeah, like we helped each other with the answers.

JUSTIN: Like a group effort pop quiz.

LUIS: Yeah. Team work.

MRS. MOORE: Well, that's just wonderful!

ETHAN: It is?

MRS. MOORE: Yes. I appreciate your effort and honesty. *(To ETHAN.)* And I appreciate you, Ethan, for teaching my class. So maybe my guidance has sunk in after all. Okay, class, what's that saying?

ALL: There are no neutral moments.

MRS. MOORE: Perfect. Make every day, every moment, every decision count! Now, class, I'm going to give you free time until the bell rings! *(They cheer. ETHAN takes a seat as LUIS puts his head down for a nap. ALEXIS takes out her makeup. LAUREN goes to play with ALEXIS'S hair, and JUSTIN pulls out his phone and bag of chips. After a moment.)* Pop quiz! *(ALL freeze and look at her. She laughs.)* Joking! Just joking! *(LIGHTS FADE to BLACK.)*

GUARDIAN ANGEL

CAST OF CHARACTERS
SETH (M)...accident-prone young man
GUARDIAN ANGEL (E).......................Seth's guardian angel

SETTING
A busy street corner.
PROPERTIES
Cell phone.

LIGHTS UP on SETH, walking, texting, and not paying attention to where he is going. As he is about to step off the curb, GUARDIAN ANGEL comes up behind him and grabs the back of his shirt to stop him.

SETH: *(Looks up to see a car speed by.)* Whoa! What the heck?! Did you see that?

GUARDIAN ANGEL: Of course, I did.

SETH: But you... you just saved my life! That car almost ran me over!

GUARDIAN ANGEL: Yep. Walking, texting, not paying attention... as usual. You almost walked right in front of that car.

SETH: *(Looks at his phone.)* Yeah... Well, thank you! Really, if it weren't for you right now, I'd be a goner. You were like my... my guardian angel!

GUARDIAN ANGEL: I am.

SETH: What?

GUARDIAN ANGEL: I am.

SETH: You are what?

GUARDIAN ANGEL: Your Guardian Angel.

SETH: And I thank you... uh... guardian angel.

GUARDIAN ANGEL: I'm serious.

SETH: And I seriously thank you from the bottom of my heart... What is your name?

GUARDIAN ANGEL: Guardian Angel.

SETH: No, seriously.

GUARDIAN ANGEL: Seriously.

SETH: *(Looks around, then laughs nervously.)* Well, thanks again. *(Turns to go.)*

GUARDIAN ANGEL: Hey, remember that time you tripped on the gravel and ripped your knee to shreds?

SETH: Uh, yeah...?

GUARDIAN ANGEL: And you had to go to the ER and have several rocks ᴅug out of your flesh. I think you got a half-dozen stitches.

SETH: How do you know about that?

GUARDIAN ANGEL: *(Sticks his foot out as if tripping him.)* I was there.

SETH: You were there?

GUARDIAN ANGEL: Unbeknownst to you, a rattlesnake was just down that path and would have bitten you. *(Smiles.)* My opponent.

SETH: Your opponent?

GUARDIAN ANGEL: Yes! That snake is my enemy. You know. Good versus Evil. Tell me you know which one I am.

SETH: Who are you?

GUARDIAN ANGEL: I told you. Your Guardian Angel.

SETH: Right. Right.

GUARDIAN ANGEL: Lucky for you, you got a smart one. And did I mention athletically inclined, witty, and, might we add— *(Slicks his hair back.)* —good looking?

SETH: You're nuts! You weren't there when I was on that trail in Arizona. There's no way.

GUARDIAN ANGEL: *(Sticks out one foot.)* Oh, I was there. Believe me, I was there.

SETH: And you're saying that you tripped me and made me fall?

GUARDIAN ANGEL: Only to save your life.

SETH: I don't believe you. Who are you?

GUARDIAN ANGEL: And remember that time in high school when you tried to ask Jennifer to the dance, but the words just wouldn't come out of your mouth? *(Puts his hand over SETH'S mouth.)* I was doing this to you.

SETH: *(Pushes him away.)* Stop!

GUARDIAN ANGEL: Sorry. Just a little trip down memory lane.

SETH: I do remember that. Somehow, I just couldn't get the words out.

GUARDIAN ANGEL: You should thank me.

SETH: Thank you? Thank you?!

GUARDIAN ANGEL: She would've said no. Actually, it wouldn't have been that nice. It would've been more like, "Only in your dreams, Seth!" So, I saved you from yourself.

SETH: That's not true! Jennifer would've said yes!

GUARDIAN ANGEL: Sorry, buddy. But, no.

SETH: You don't know that! You're just some weird psycho person who's following me around for some unknown reason!

GUARDIAN ANGEL: Oh! Oh! Oh! Remember that time in junior high when you got stuck in the boy's restroom?

SETH: How do you know about that?

GUARDIAN ANGEL: Because I was the one holding the door shut, again saving you from a near disaster.

SETH: What disaster?

GUARDIAN ANGEL: The Wilson twins wanted to teach you a lesson. They were looking for you.

SETH: For that prank I pulled on them in the lunchroom?

GUARDIAN ANGEL: That's right. Dumb, dumb, dumb...

SETH: What?

GUARDIAN ANGEL: Replacing the white creamy middle of a chocolate sandwich cookie with toothpaste? Dumb, dumb, dumb...

SETH: I was in junior high! Junior high kids do dumb stuff!

GUARDIAN ANGEL: That's no exaggeration. Well, anyway, the Wilson boys were on their way to teach you a lesson, but I, being the observant and compassionate guardian angel that I am, spared you from getting a single scratch.

SETH: I'm not a coward!

GUARDIAN ANGEL: They would have eaten you for lunch.

SETH: No. I would've taken them down! Without a scratch on me.

GUARDIAN ANGEL: *(Laughs.)* Like Jennifer would have said, in your dreams.

SETH: Stop it! You weren't there!

GUARDIAN ANGEL: "Let me out! Let me out! Help! Help!" But I held that door shut.

SETH: That wasn't you!

GUARDIAN ANGEL: "Someone let me out! Please!" Good thing the Wilson twins didn't hear you screaming. "Someone help me! Help me! I can't breathe! I can't breathe in here!"

SETH: *(Angry.)* Who are you?

GUARDIAN ANGEL: And remember that time you tried to launch a homemade bottle rocket? Again, dumb idea. Dumb, dumb, dumb.

SETH: How do you know about that?

GUARDIAN ANGEL: Thanks to my bravery, that bottle rocket fizzled out on the ground instead of catching your parents' house on fire!

SETH: That was you?

GUARDIAN ANGEL: Plus, you would've caught your hair on fire.

SETH: But that rocket was for a science project. It was going to be so cool.

GUARDIAN ANGEL: Cool to suffer third degree burns over half your body?

SETH: But... you?

GUARDIAN ANGEL: Yep! Go me! I saved the day. As usual. Do you want to thank me now?

SETH: *(Reaches out to touch him.)* Whoa! I can see you, but I can't feel you!

GUARDIAN ANGEL: I'm invisible too. Well, to everyone but you right now.

SETH: How is this possible?

GUARDIAN ANGEL: I thought a little gratitude was in order. You've put me through a lot, you know? Playing on the train tracks, the bull riding adventure, hang gliding over the cliffs with your own contraption, shark hunting... Oh, and remember that time you had the great idea to jump into a swimming pool... with no water!

SETH: I was going to land on a mattress! Well, that was the plan.

GUARDIAN ANGEL: Two words, major head injury.

SETH: That's three words.

GUARDIAN ANGEL: Whatever.

SETH: Oh, great! I have a guardian angel with an attitude.

GUARDIAN ANGEL: Learned it from you. So, how about a little gratitude here? You've made my job very difficult, you know?

SETH: How about this? I free you. You are free to leave me and look after someone else.

GUARDIAN ANGEL: Really? You really want to live your life without a guardian angel?

SETH: I'll be fine.

GUARDIAN ANGEL: I wouldn't count on it. Not with all your great ideas!

SETH: I'm sure. Your services are no longer needed. So, poof and be gone! *(Pause.)* Go, I said! *(GUARDIAN ANGEL pushes him.)* Why did you do that?

GUARDIAN ANGEL: One last time for old time's sake.

SETH: What do you mean?

GUARDIAN ANGEL: You know, pushing you out of the way of dangerous situations.

SETH: Well, your services are no longer needed!

GUARDIAN ANGEL: I wouldn't be so sure about that, if I was you.

SETH: I'm sure.

GUARDIAN ANGEL: Because this afternoon... well, never mind. *(Turns to go.)*

SETH: What? What?

GUARDIAN ANGEL: Maybe you can join my team after today.

SETH: What team?

GUARDIAN ANGEL: Become a guardian angel. I wonder who you'll get to follow around all day? *(Points.)* Maybe him.

SETH: Him? That old man with the tattoo?

GUARDIAN ANGEL: *(Points.)* Or her.

SETH: The mother of three?

GUARDIAN ANGEL: And no sleeping on the job. You must be alert at all times.

SETH: Why would I become a guardian angel this afternoon?

GUARDIAN ANGEL: Well, since you've let me go... and after the upcoming incident this afternoon... *(Pats him.)* Maybe you'll be on my team! Team 472013. That's my team. And might I add, we've had one of the least mistakes known to human kind.

SETH: Mistakes?

GUARDIAN ANGEL: Late interferences. Not paying attention and saving people in time. I take my job very seriously! Well, most of the time. I did fail you once.

SETH: When?

GUARDIAN ANGEL: Remember that choking incident when you were eating the breakfast burrito? I clearly was not paying attention. Thank goodness your friend Joe stepped in. A little Heimlich maneuver and you were good to go. Sorry about that.

SETH: What were you doing?

GUARDIAN ANGEL: Talking to my friend, Cosima. She has the most beautiful long hair, big beautiful eyes, a smile to die for... Well, not you. I keep you from that. But, wow, does she make my heart flip-flop. So, my heart was flip-flopping while you were choking on your burrito. Again, sorry about that.

SETH: Well, like I said. Your services are no longer needed. I can take care of myself, thank you very much.

GUARDIAN ANGEL: You'll be sorry!

SETH: No, I don't think so.

GUARDIAN ANGEL: Well, okay, then. I'm out of here. *(EXITS.)*

SETH: *(Calls OFF.)* Great. See ya. *(Thinks.)* But... I wonder what's going to happen to me this afternoon. Something's supposed to happen. Well, that's just dumb. I'm being dumb. Nothing is going to happen. *(Thinks. Calls OFF.)* Wait! Wait! Come back! I've changed my mind about firing you. Come back! *(Thinks.)* I know! I'm going to go home, crawl into bed, put the sheets over my head, and stay there all day! *(Rushes OFF.)*

GUARDIAN ANGEL: *(ENTERS, having not heard SETH.)* What does he think he's doing? He can't fire me! And when that ceiling fan breaks loose from the ceiling, I'll be there to spare his life. Again. As always. Over and over again. Go me. *(Sighs.)* I need a raise. *(Starts to run OFF after SETH.)* Wait for me! You can't get through your life without me! *(He's OUT. BLACKOUT.)*

LOVE AT FIRST SIGHT

CAST OF CHARACTERS

SARA (F) .... recently single
RYAN (M) .... a good guy
JED (M) .... Sara's ex-boyfriend
CAMI (F) .... married passer-by
DARCY (F) .... another passer-by
KACI (F) .... Jed's new fling
EXTRAS .... mall shoppers

SETTING
A mall food court.

PROPERTIES
Tables with chairs. Pizza slice on a plate, two shopping bags.

LIGHTS UP on RYAN sitting at a table eating pizza in a mall food court. SARA rushes IN and sits down across from him.

SARA: *(Breathless.)* Hurry! Act like you know me!

RYAN: Uh…okay. It's great to see you again. *(Leans in and whispers.)* Even though we've never met before in our entire lives. But now that you're here, I can honestly say that I'm glad we've met.

SARA: *(Looks over her shoulder.)* Okay, now I need you to act like you're in love with me!

RYAN: Shouldn't we exchange names first?

SARA: *(Quickly.)* Sure! Hi! I'm Sara!

RYAN: Hi, Sara. I'm Ryan. *(Offers his hand.)*

SARA: *(Takes his hand and squeezes it tight.)* Could you keep holding my hand? Like you want to hold my hand? Like you never want to let go of my hand?

RYAN: Well, sure, but could you relax a bit? You're cutting off my circulation.

SARA: Oh, sorry. *(Looks back.)* Hurry! Pretend you're in love with me!

RYAN: Is this a game? Like Truth or Dare?

SARA: Yes. Sort of. And if you help me out, I'll buy you a double scoop of your favorite ice cream from over there.

RYAN: You got it! *(Kisses her hand.)* I love you.

SARA: Don't stop. Keep going.

RYAN: Let me just say this. There's nowhere I'd rather be than at this food court with my one and only... stranger... that I've never met in my entire life. And if I might add... you're beautiful.

SARA: I am?

RYAN: Yes, you are.

SARA: In real life or pretend? Oh, never mind. I'll pretend you meant that in real life. That'll help this whole fake relationship seem real.

RYAN: I meant it.

SARA: *(Glances back.)* Okay, he's coming! Don't forget! I'm buying you ice cream to pretend you're in love with me.

RYAN: Two scoops?

SARA: Two scoops. So, go! Go!

RYAN: Go? You want me to leave?

SARA: No! Go ahead with your adoring me.

RYAN: Oh, of course. Well, Sara, you have a charming personality.

SARA: In real life or pretend? Oh, never mind.

RYAN: In real life. *(JED ENTERS.)*

SARA: *(Laughs.)* You're so funny! I love the way you make me laugh! I don't know when I've ever been so happy!

JED: Yesterday. You were never happier yesterday. Remember?

SARA: *(Glances back.)* Oh, it's you. Hi, Jed.

RYAN: Hi. *(Offers his hand.)* I'm Ryan. Her...uh...her...

SARA: New boyfriend!

RYAN: That's it! Yeah! I'm her new boyfriend.

JED: That was fast.

SARA: Well, life goes on.

RYAN: Yes, it was fast. But I guess you could say it's like that old saying, "Love at first sight."

JED: Are you kidding me? Love at first sight?

SARA: *(To RYAN.)* You're kidding, right?

JED: Well, I can do that too!

SARA: Do what?

JED: Find someone to fall in love with me at first sight! And why not? I'm good-looking, charming, funny—

SARA: Don't leave out a big flirt!

RYAN: Well, you can't really force it. It must happen naturally. You must allow the winds of destiny to deliver your one true love to you as an unexpected blessing.

SARA: That was romantic.

JED: Oh, I can be romantic too!

SARA: In a flirty kind of way. With every girl out there.

RYAN: Your boyfriend's a flirt?

SARA: My ex-boyfriend's a flirt. *(CAMI ENTERS and walks by, carrying a shopping bag.)*

JED: Hey, hey, hey!

CAMI: *(Stops.)* Excuse me?

JED: Hey, beautiful.

CAMI: Do I know you?

JED: You do now. *(Offers his hand.)* I'm Jed.

CAMI: *(Refuses to take his hand.)* Why were you yelling at me?

JED: Let me ask you this. Do you believe in love at first sight?

CAMI: Yes.

JED: *(Shoots SARA a look.)* Uh-huh! See? *(To CAMI.)* Me too!

CAMI: That's what happened between me and my husband. *(Points OFF.)* He's right over there. Would you like to meet him?

JED: Uh… *(Looks OFF and waves.)* You've got a real keeper here, sir! *(To CAMI.)* Sorry. I'm just being dumb today.

CAMI: It's okay. See ya.

JED: Bye. *(CAMI EXITS.)*

SARA: That was real smooth, Jed.

JED: Little mistake. Little mistake. *(DARCY ENTERS and walks by with a shopping bag.)* Hey, beautiful!

DARCY: Are you talking to me?

JED: Yes, I'm talking to you. You're beautiful.

DARCY: Do you want to die?

JED: Excuse me?

DARCY: My boyfriend is right over there. *(Points OFF.)*

JED: You have a boyfriend?

DARCY: Yes. And do you want me to tell him how beautiful you think I am?

JED: Uh, no! No! Sorry! You, uh... looked like someone else. Yes! That's it! I confused you with someone else!

DARCY: Apparently! *(Flips around and EXITS.)*

RYAN: Yep. It's hard finding love at first sight. *(Takes SARA'S hand.)* But we were lucky. As lucky as they come.

SARA: You mean it? *(Snaps out of it.)* I mean, yes! Who knew it'd happen so fast?

RYAN: I sure didn't. Five minutes ago, I was scarfing down a slice of cheese pizza, and then you walked into my life.

JED: *(To SARA.)* So, it's over? Just like that?

SARA: What do you mean "just like that"? You were the one sending heart emoticons to a girl at work, which in my eyes, is cheating on me!

JED: I wasn't cheating. I was flirting. There's a difference.

RYAN: Oh, that's not good, dude.

JED: And I'm sorry, Sara. It was a stupid thing to do.

RYAN: Yeah, very stupid.

JED: I guess I was weak.

RYAN: Or dumb.

JED: Kaci was texting me, and I got drawn into it.

RYAN: Likely excuse.

JED: But I learned my lesson!

SARA: Again? This isn't the first time I caught you flirting with other girls. How do you think that makes me feel?

RYAN: I would never do that to you.

SARA: You wouldn't?

RYAN: Never.

JED: I'm an idiot.

RYAN: *(To JED.)* Man, you can't flirt with other girls if you're in a relationship. If you're single, sure. Then you can send a little wink, virtual or real.

SARA: Oh, he winks at other girls too.

JED: Only if they're cute.

RYAN: *(To SARA.)* Why did you put up with that?

SARA: Good question. Why did I?

JED: Sara, I apologize! I realize I've been stupid.

RYAN: It takes a strong man to apologize.

JED: Thank you.

RYAN: But it takes a stronger woman to leave a bad relationship.

SARA: Very true.

JED: Sara, let's just put this behind us. Give me a chance to show you that I'm a changed man. No more flirting or kissing other girls. I promise. Cross my heart.

SARA: *(Jumps up.)* You kissed other girls?

JED: No! I mean, yes! I mean… What do I mean? I mean, it was a dumb thing to do, and now I've seen the error of my ways!

SARA: *(Plops back down.)* It's over.

RYAN: Good decision.

JED: But I'm sorry! And the hearts I sent to Kaci only meant that I loved her new haircut… and her new outfit… and those cute little glasses she wears… and those little freckles on her nose… *(SARA screams. Suddenly, KACI runs IN and throws her arms around JED.)*

KACI: Jed! Oh, Jed! I've missed you! It's so good to see you! Why didn't you text me back last night? Did you fall asleep? I liked those little hearts you sent!

JED: Uh… this is, uh…

KACI: Hi! I'm Kaci!

SARA: Hi. I'm Sara. Jed's ex-girlfriend.

KACI: Oh, yeah. He told me you two weren't happy. You know, sometimes relationships just don't work out.

SARA: That's true. *(JED gets distracted by another woman passing by [on or off stage].)*

KACI: Isn't that true, Jed? Jed? Jed? Who are you looking at?

SARA: He's winking.

KACI: Who's he winking at?

SARA: Other girls. He likes to flirt. A lot. So as long as you're okay with that, I'm sure things will work out just great.

KACI: *(Glares at Jed.)* I'm not okay with that! Jed? Jed? Did you hear me? I'm not okay with that!

JED: *(Still with his eye on the other girl.)* What? What?

KACI: I said I'm not okay with that!

JED: What? I wasn't doing anything.

KACI: Don't lie to me! I saw you flirting with that girl over there!

JED: No. I was just being friendly. *(Blows a kiss to the other girl.)*

KACI: *(Shakes her head.)* Forget it! *(To SARA.)* He's all yours! *(EXITS.)*

JED: Hey, where are you going? Okay, well, I'll text you later. Okay?

RYAN: *(Leans in.)* I've always liked the name Sara.

SARA: Really?

JED: Hey, Sara, I'm going over there to talk to that girl in the red jacket. I saw her smiling at me. I think she wants to get to know me better. *(Starts to go.)* And who wouldn't want to get to know me better? I'm a very likable guy. Not to mention charming and handsome! *(EXITS. From OFFSTAGE.)* Hello, beautiful!

SARA: Thanks.

RYAN: For what?

SARA: Coming to my rescue. *(Takes out her wallet.)* And now I owe you.

RYAN: No, don't worry about it.

SARA: But I keep my promises.

RYAN: So do I.

SARA: And I promised to buy you some ice cream for acting like you love me.

RYAN: Absolutely not! It's on me. I'll buy you ice cream. And besides, that was fun. I actually enjoyed it. And I'm also glad to see you get away from that jerk.

SARA: Well, thank you. It was a long time coming.

RYAN: *(Reaches out and touches her hand.)* You are beautiful. And yes, in real life.

SARA: Wow. Thank you.

RYAN: So tell me, do you believe in love at first sight?

SARA: I can't say I ever did, but...

RYAN: But?

SARA: I think it might be possible.

RYAN: Me too. *(They smile.)* Can I buy you a double scoop of ice cream?

SARA: Yes. I'd like that.

RYAN: Me too. *(LIGHTS FADE to BLACK.)*

NO SOLICITORS ALLOWED

CAST OF CHARACTERS

ELAINE (F) .... woman wary of scams
HAROLD (M) .... door-to-door salesman

SETTING
Elaine's front porch.

PROPERTIES
Porch bench, door with wreath and sign that reads "No Solicitors Allowed," potted plants. Small jar, goofy hat, name tag, coupon.

LIGHTS UP on ELAINE standing on her front porch, already irritated with HAROLD. HAROLD smiles constantly, wears a goofy hat, and holds up a small jar. A porch bench sits RIGHT, surrounded by potted plants. A wreath hangs on the door.

ELAINE: Let me say this one more time before I call the police. Get off my property!

HAROLD: Ma'am, if you would just listen to what I have to say. If you don't agree that this Miracle Stress Relief Cream with Essential Oils is the best product you've ever seen, then I will leave. No questions asked.

ELAINE: Can you not read? Do you not see the sign posted at my front door? No solicitors allowed!

HAROLD: But, ma'am, I'm not a solicitor.

ELAINE: Excuse me! Aren't you trying to sell me something?

HAROLD: No, ma'am!

ELAINE: Then why are you here?

HAROLD: Ma'am, I'm only here to educate you on this revolutionary cream that works to calm your inner self. Massage this on your temples, under your nose, or on certain pressure points, and all stress melts away. Plus, it helps with depression, fatigue, anxiety—

ELAINE: *(Yells.)* Excuse me! Do I look stressed? Do I?

HAROLD: You look quite lovely, ma'am, if I might say.

ELAINE: Flattery will get you nowhere!

HAROLD: Ma'am, I'm not here to sell you anything. My only goal is to introduce you to this Miracle Stress Relief Cream. Is it safe and natural? Yes, it is.

ELAINE: I didn't ask, did I?

HAROLD: Effective while moisturizing the skin? Yes. Strengthens the body's ability to deal with stress? Yes, it does!

ELAINE: If I appear stressed, it's because you're making me stressed. You! If you don't mind, please leave. Shall I spell it out for you? L-E-A-V-E! Or in simple terms, G-O!

HAROLD: I simply want you to try this wonderful cream.

ELAINE: Why? So I'll buy it?

HAROLD: No, ma'am.

ELAINE: Liar. *(Taunts.)* Liar, liar pants on fire! Actually, I'd like to see your pants catch on fire. I wonder if I would even bother to grab the garden hose.

HAROLD: Ma'am, I would never lie to you. Cross my heart. *(Crosses his heart.)*

ELAINE: *(Holds out her hand.)* Go ahead. Hand it over.

HAROLD: What?

ELAINE: My free gift.

HAROLD: Your free gift is available once I've completed my demonstration of this Miracle Stress Relief Cream.

ELAINE: Let's see, the vacuum cleaner salesman offered to clean my carpet. The spot remover guy wanted to clean the rust off my driveway. What do you want to do? Rub that stuff all over my hand?

HAROLD: If I might. May I?

ELAINE: You may not!

HAROLD: Ma'am, this Miracle Stress Relief Cream with Essential Oils is the best calming potion in the world.

ELAINE: And you're selling it door-to-door?

HAROLD: I'm not here to sell anything.

ELAINE: Sure, sure. If this product is so amazing, why don't you do an infomercial instead? You know, something I can watch at three a.m. when I can't fall asleep.

HAROLD: This helps with insomnia as well.

ELAINE: Stop it with your sales pitch! I'm not going to buy anything from you.

HAROLD: The makers of this Miracle Stress Relief Cream believe this product is so unique that instead of the mass-market hype, we prefer to introduce our product to customers on a one-on-one basis.

ELAINE: What a scam!

HAROLD: Do you ever suffer with meltdowns where you freak out and scream? Perhaps throwing items at people you love or at strangers?

ELAINE: *(Grabs the wreath off the door and throws it at him.)* What do you think? Do I look like I'm having a meltdown? *(Pulls flowers out of a pot and throws them at him.)* Do I?

HAROLD: *(Dodges.)* You know, there are other ways to deal with stress. *(Holds out the jar.)*

ELAINE: *(Grabs more flowers and throws them at him.)* I think this feels pretty good.

HAROLD: Have you ever tried using essential oils? They make this cream special. *(Points to the jar's label.)* Look, eucalyptus and lavender essential oils. *(Opens the jar.)* Just smell. Let your mind and body relax.

ELAINE: What a joke.

HAROLD: It's true. *(Holds the jar closer to her.)* Take a whiff.

ELAINE: I don't believe in that hocus pocus stuff.

HAROLD: No hocus pocus here. It's genuine. Genuine Miracle Stress Relief Cream developed by the world-renowned scientist Jaba Corbal—

ELAINE: Never heard of him.

HAROLD: Soon, everyone will have heard of Jaba. Trust me.

ELAINE: But I don't trust you, sorry! *(Points to her sign.)* Let me point this out to you one more time, since you obviously have trouble reading.

HAROLD: But I'm not a solicitor, I'm an ambassador.

ELAINE: I don't buy stuff from you salesmen, and I don't want you at my door. I don't trust you, and I don't like you. To top it off, I'm not stressed! Oh, I feel like pulling out my hair right now.

HAROLD: Don't be embarrassed. Everyone suffers from stress from time to time.

ELAINE: Listen here, mister...

HAROLD: I'm sorry. I failed to give you my name. *(Offers his hand.)* I'm Harold. Harold Mosby. *(Points to a nametag on his shirt.)* Top seller of the Miracle Stress Relief Cream with Essential Oils.

ELAINE: *(Refuses to shake his hand.)* Ah-ha! You just said seller.

HAROLD: I'm only here to reveal some truths to you. Just admit that you are a basket case sometimes.

ELAINE: *(Throws her arms around.)* Do I look like a basket case? Do I look like I'm about to explode and lose my mind?

HAROLD: Honestly, yes. But I sincerely want to help you.

ELAINE: I'm not stressed, Mr. Harold Mosby. What I do have is a problem with you door-to-door salesmen trying to sell me something that I don't need or want. You're interfering with my soap operas! I already missed Jason's proposal to Anna with his supposedly dead wife standing just behind the bushes. Oh, why did I answer the door? *(Wags finger in his face.)* If I missed his dead wife popping out from that bush, I'm going to be very angry with you!

HAROLD: I'm glad you brought that up. Did you know soap opera stars use this revolutionary cream by the hundreds?

ELAINE: They do not!

HAROLD: How else would they deal with the stressful situations in their characters' lives? The stress of proposing to a beautiful woman as the wife appears from out of nowhere, the stress of accepting a proposal from the love of your life only to have his dead wife show up at that very moment, not to mention memorizing all those lines. *(Holds out the jar.)* I'm telling you, they use this stuff.

ELAINE: Seriously?

HAROLD: Seriously! I'm telling you the truth. For an introductory price, which is only guaranteed for today, you can purchase a jar of this Miracle Stress Relief Cream with Essential Oils. But wait! Let's not get ahead of this spectacular offer. We haven't even discussed your free gift.

ELAINE: Finally! What is it? A nail file? A little magnet for my fridge with your phone number on it?

HAROLD: A coupon!

ELAINE: A coupon?

HAROLD: That's right! Here you go. *(Hands her a coupon.)*

ELAINE: *(Reads, unimpressed.)* Twenty dollars off?

HAROLD: Twenty dollars off your first jar of Miracle Stress Relief Cream, which means your first order will only cost you $99.99. Is that an incredible offer, or what?

ELAINE: Are you crazy? A hundred dollars for a stupid cream?

HAROLD: Did I mention that any additional orders will include free shipping?

ELAINE: You must think I'm an idiot. Who would buy a cream for over a hundred dollars?

HAROLD: Not with the coupon! Just $99.99. Oh, and I left out the best part. For no extra fee, we'll throw in a sample of our Stress Relief Body Wash as well.

ELAINE: Oh, the thrill.

HAROLD: How many jars would you like to buy?

ELAINE: You forgot something.

HAROLD: What's that?

ELAINE: My demonstration!

HAROLD: Oh, but of course. *(Opens the jar.)* Hold out your wrist, please.

ELAINE: *(Holds out her wrist.)* Why not? I've wasted this much time already.

HAROLD: *(Rubs the cream into her wrist.)* Feel the smooth texture? The tingle? That's the miracle potion going right to work.

ELAINE: It does tingle.

HAROLD: Now put your wrist up to your nose and take a deep breath.

ELAINE: This is stupid. I don't know why I'm doing this. I know it's not going to work. *(Smells her wrist, then calms.)* Oh... wow. *(Takes another whiff.)* Could you put some of that under my nose?

HAROLD: Certainly. *(Dabs under her nose.)* Try that. I think you'll like it.

ELAINE: Oh, my... Mr. Mosby, this is just wonderful. *(Smiles at him.)* I like your hat. Did I tell you that? It's very becoming on you.

HAROLD: *(Touches his hat and smiles.)* Why, thank you.

ELAINE: You're so welcome. *(Takes a deep breath.)* Oh, what a beautiful day it is. Do you hear those precious little birds chirping? I love their songs. They just make me happy.

HAROLD: I see that.

ELAINE: The sky is so blue.

HAROLD: Yes.

ELAINE: *(Another deep breath.)* The air is so fresh.

HAROLD: Yes, it is.

ELAINE: Do you like coffee?

HAROLD: Well, yes.

ELAINE: Why don't you come inside, and I'll give you a cup. While I'm getting it ready, you can tally up how much I owe you. I'd like two jars, please. And if you could sign me up for automatic shipments once a month, that would be lovely.

HAROLD: Certainly.

ELAINE: *(Turns, sees the sign, and tears it off.)* Please, come inside. Do you like cream and sugar?

HAROLD: Sure, thank you. *(LIGHTS FADE to BLACK.)*

———————o———————

BEST ACTRESS

CAST OF CHARACTERS

HOST (E) ....confused award announcer
CAMILLE (F)..amateur actress
STAGE MANAGER (E) ....intense problem-solver
EMILY (F)... another actress

SETTING
A community theatre awards ceremony at Midtown Hall.

PROPERTIES
Podium with microphone and trophy. Notecard, plain sealed envelope, sealed envelope with a red star.

LIGHTS UP on our HOST, standing behind a podium in formal wear. He holds a notecard and a sealed envelope. A trophy sits on the podium.

HOST: And the award for Best Actress in a ten-minute play is… *(Opens envelope.)* Camille Hodges!

CAMILLE: *(Rushes ON from the audience and grabs the trophy.)* Thank you! Thank you, thank you, thank you! *(Turns to the HOST.)* Oh, thank you! *(To the AUDIENCE.)* Thank you all so much. This has been the role of a lifetime for me!

HOST: *(Gives her a strange look.)* Performing in a ten-minute play was the role of a lifetime?

CAMILLE: *(Ignores him.)* Flush It Down the Toilet was written for me! As my character says in the play… *(Dramatic.)* "It's not until you push the lever that you take control of your life!"

HOST: *(Gives her a strange look.)* By flushing the toilet? *(To the AUDIENCE.)* Well, okay. Camille Hodges, best actress in a ten-minute play.

CAMILLE: *(Moves closer to the microphone.)* This award means so much to me! I'd like to thank the director, Landon Giles. And of course, the writer, Nancy Hawkins. My high school drama teacher, Mrs. Shields, for believing in me. Mrs. Peterson, my third grade teacher, for giving me my first role as Small Child in Crowd. Sure, it was not a speaking part, but that's when I knew I was destined to be a star! I'd also like to thank my best friend, Haley, for always encouraging me, my ex-boyfriend, Dustin, for breaking my heart so I could feel the pain I needed for this role of a lifetime, my mom, my dad... and my unborn children! Thank you! Thank you! Thank you! I love you all!

HOST: Your unborn children?

STAGE MANAGER: *(ENTERS with an envelope and crosses to CAMILLE.)* I'm sorry to do this, but... *(Snatches the trophy away from her. To the HOST. Sotto voce.)* You were supposed to grab the envelope with the red star!

HOST: What? *(Looks at the envelope.)*

STAGE MANAGER: The winners are in the red-starred envelopes.

HOST: But no one told me that!

STAGE MANAGER: Well, of course they told you that!

HOST: No, they didn't!

STAGE MANAGER: At awards program meeting? Attendance was mandatory.

HOST: Well, uh... I was busy. I had, you know, stuff to take care of. Actually, it was my Love Bird. Her little tweet sounded off. I knew something was wrong. So I had to rush Tweety to the vet. Tweety didn't make it. *(Cries.)* Tweety is now—well, I hope—flying her little heart away up there. *(Wipes his eyes.)* Oh, Tweety...

STAGE MANAGER: *(Grabs the HOST'S envelope.)* This envelope is plain and white. No red star here, is there? No winner here! *(Holds up the red-starred envelope.)* This is the winning envelope.

CAMILLE: What are you saying?

STAGE MANAGER: I'm saying there has been a mistake.

CAMILLE: A mistake? No!

HOST: I'm sorry, but no one told me to look for the red-starred envelope.

STAGE MANAGER: We did tell everyone, but you were too busy with your dying bird.

HOST: Well, I'm sorry! *(Wipes his eyes.)* I loved that bird!

STAGE MANAGER: When you signed up for this, you agreed to attend the mandatory meeting. And when you didn't, you missed the most important information of all—only pick up the red-starred envelope!

HOST: Well, excuse me! But why would you even bother to put the loser's name in an envelope? What's the point of that?

CAMILLE: *(Tries to nudge closer to the microphone.)* Can I continue with my acceptance speech?

STAGE MANAGER: *(Ignores her. To HOST.)* Because every nominee is placed inside a special envelope, and when the votes are tallied, the winner gets the red star. And the losers get a... well, nothing.

HOST: *(Holds up his envelope.)* Wow. So, this is a loser envelope.

CAMILLE: What? Give me my trophy!

STAGE MANAGER: *(To CAMILLE.)* I apologize for the confusion. *(To HOST.)* Here's the winning envelope.

HOST: Thank you. *(STAGE MANAGER EXITS.)*

CAMILLE: *(Into the microphone.)* And I'd like to thank Tommy Newby for directing my play in the garage in fifth grade. You saw my potential even back then. You said, "Camille—"

HOST: You need to step aside. You're not the winner after all.

CAMILLE: Oh, yes, I am!

HOST: No, you're not. If we may continue... The winner for Best Actress in a ten-minute play is... *(Opens red-starred envelope.)* Emily Locke!

EMILY: *(Rushes ON from the AUDIENCE.)* Oh, my goodness. I can't believe this!

CAMILLE: *(Grabs the trophy. Into the microphone.)* And I'd also like to thank my cat, Tiny. Tiny, you were there for me when I memorized my lines, and without you... without your purrs of encouragement...

EMILY: *(To HOST.)* Can you please remove her so I can give my acceptance speech?

HOST: Camille, please. If you could just step aside...

CAMILLE: *(Dramatic.)* And I want to thank you. Yes, you, for supporting the theatres! Because without you, I would not be here.

HOST: Ms. Hodges, please. You are not the winner.

CAMILLE: And God! How could I forget to thank God?

HOST: Ms. Hodges, please! Please step away from the microphone. The best actress in a ten-minute play is Emily Locke.

EMILY: That's right, Camille. Step aside! *(Pushes CAMILLE out of the way.)* I knew there had to be a mistake. My performance in the ten-minute version of *Macbeth* was brilliant. "Out damn spot! Out, I say!"

CAMILLE: *(Grabs the microphone.)* And last, I'd like to thank myself.

HOST: Ms. Hodges, if you would please let me escort you off the stage.

EMILY: *(Pushes in to the microphone. Glares at CAMILLE.)* "Out, damned spot! Out, I say!"

HOST: *(To EMILY.)* My sincerest apologies. No one told me to look for the red-starred envelope.

CAMILLE: *(Into the microphone.)* Oh! Oh, oh, oh! And I'd also like to thank—

EMILY: Stop! Will you just stop? I am the winner! Not you! So please, just step aside and give me my trophy.

CAMILLE: And one last shout-out to my fish, Bubbles.

EMILY: Really? Your fish? *(To the HOST.)* Can you not have her removed? Call security?

CAMILLE: And a shout-out to all the other nominees. You are all amazing out there, and I feel honored to have won this. And believe me, I understand the pressure and extreme dedication it takes to perform in a ten-minute play. The rehearsals, the memorization of lines, blocking, going over and over and over it until you get it right... *(Lifts the award.)* So, this means the world to me!

EMILY: Enough already! Give me my trophy!

CAMILLE: *(Into the microphone.)* And a special shout-out to Emily Locke.

EMILY: You don't have to give a shout-out to me because I'm standing right here! And I'm the winner, not you! Hello!

HOST: Security!

EMILY: Security! We need you onstage immediately!

HOST: *(Looks OFFSTAGE.)* What? Oh, okay. *(To the AUDIENCE.)* Well, they say we have to wrap it up. *(Looks at his watch.)* We're out of time.

CAMILLE: *(Leans into the microphone.)* So, lastly, I'd like to thank you, Emily.

EMILY: You don't get to thank anyone, because you lost! Can you not get that through your thick head?

CAMILLE: No. I won.

EMILY: No. You lost.

CAMILLE: Won.

EMILY: Lost.

CAMILLE: Won!

EMILY: Lost!

CAMILLE: *(Smiles at the AUDIENCE.)* We all heard the Host announce my name, and there are no take-backs in theatre. What happens onstage, stays onstage. In other words, you only get one chance to get it right. Because this isn't TV, and you can't have a re-do. This is live! And we all heard the Host call my name. Camille Hodges for Best Actress in a ten-minute play. So anyway, thank you for your support, Emily. It means the world to me. And for being here with me. For wanting what I have, but knowing you can't have it. So, thank you. *(To the AUDIENCE.)* Thank you, thank you, thank you! *(EXITS with the trophy.)*

EMILY: *(To HOST.)* Go get her! Go get my trophy!

HOST: *(Looks OFFSTAGE.)* I know. I know.

EMILY: You know what?

HOST: We're out of time. *(To the AUDIENCE.)* And what an evening this has been, hasn't it, folks?

EMILY: *(Pushes him away from the microphone.)* No! It's my turn! It's my turn to thank the audience.

HOST: There's no time left. *(To the AUDIENCE.)* Have a wonderful evening my friends, supporters of theatre. Good night. *(EXITS. LIGHTS DIM.)*

EMILY: Wait! Where is everyone going? I'm not done! I have people to thank! Can you just wait? Can you sit back down? I'm the winner of the Best Actress award in a ten-minute play. Me! Why are you leaving? This is my moment. *(Taps the microphone.)* Did you turn this off? Hello? Can you hear me? *(Talks louder.)* I have several people I'd like to thank tonight. *(Pulls out a long sheet of paper.)* This is my cheat sheet so I wouldn't leave anyone out. First, I'd like to thank... *(LIGHTS DIM further.)* What the heck? Why did you turn off the lights? Nobody can see me now! *(Taps the microphone.)* Can you turn this back on? And the lights? Please. *(Pause.)* Okay, fine! So first, I'd like to thank Shakespeare, because without your poetic words, I could not have won this award tonight. Hello? Hello? Is anyone out there? *(BLACKOUT.)*

FINDERS KEEPERS

CAST OF CHARACTERS

SARA (F) ....older teen
MOM (F)... her mom
CUSTOMER ONE (E) ....passerby
CUSTOMER TWO (E).. another
PEDESTRIAN (E)... another
STORE MANAGER (E) .... voice of authority
CUSTOMER THREE (E).. another
MADISON (E)... Sara's best friend

SETTING
In front of a grocery store.
PROPERTIES
Bench. Purses, lottery ticket, penny, sack of groceries.

LIGHTS UP on MOM and SARA walking towards a grocery store. They stop at a bench. MOM carries a purse.

SARA: Hey, Mom, can I just hang out here while you go shopping? I know how you like to go up and down every aisle. And stop and read the labels. *(Mimics.)* Calories, one ninety. Fat, fourteen grams. Sodium, nine hundred forty. Oh, no, no, no, no! Too much salt. *(Pretends to put the item back on shelf and sits down on the bench.)* I'll just sit here and enjoy some fresh air instead.

MOM: That's fine. I'll get what we need for spaghetti tonight and be right back.

SARA: Don't forget the French bread. I can make some garlic toast.

MOM: Sounds good. Back in a few. *(EXITS into the store. SARA looks around, then down at her feet. Mindlessly, she* *picks up a lottery scratch-off ticket from the ground and looks at it.)*

SARA: *(Suddenly alert.)* This can't be! Can it? *(Looks closer. Reads.)* "Scratch off three money bags and win fifty thousand dollars!" One. Two. Three! There are three money bags! *(Looks around, at the ground, and back at the ticket. CUSTOMER ONE ENTERS, heading to the store. SARA jumps up.)* Excuse me! Hey! Excuse me! Did you drop something?

CUSTOMER ONE: *(Looks around and checks his pockets.)* No, I don't think so.

SARA: You weren't coming back here to look for it?

CUSTOMER ONE: It?

SARA: Worth a lot of money?!

CUSTOMER ONE: A lot of money? *(Laughs.)* That's something I don't have. But I get by. And let me tell you, the generic brand in there is just as good. I can't tell a difference, except at the checkout. *(Considers her.)* Did you lose something?

SARA: No. I found something.

CUSTOMER ONE: What?

SARA: I... uh... nothing. Are you sure you didn't lose something?

CUSTOMER ONE: I'm sure. So, what did you find? Wait! Let me guess. A twenty-dollar bill? Hey, keep it. I say finders keepers. If people can't hold onto their stuff and there's no way of finding out who it belongs to, then I say it's your lucky day. So, keep it.

SARA: Really?

CUSTOMER ONE: Does it have anyone's name on it?

SARA: No, but...

CUSTOMER ONE: Then it's your lucky day. Well, I better go get my shopping done. Generic. All generic. But it's all the same to me, except for the price. *(EXITS into the store as CUSTOMER TWO ENTERS from the store, dragging her feet and looking at the ground.)*

SARA: *(Sees her and assumes.)* You lost something, didn't you?

CUSTOMER TWO: No, but I did step in some gum. *(Stops to look at the bottom of her foot.)* Ugh! Don't you just hate that? *(Attempts to scrape it off.)*

SARA: I do, but… You didn't lose anything?

CUSTOMER TWO: My sanity! *(Lifts her foot.)* Just look at that! Why do people spit their gum out on the ground? They act like it's the trash can. Never mind who steps in it! *(Stomps her foot ridiculously.)* I hate other people's nasty gum!

SARA: Me too.

CUSTOMER TWO: *(Scrapes her foot again.)* Did you lose something?

SARA: No, I'm just waiting on my mom to finish shopping.

CUSTOMER TWO: Nice day to be outside.

SARA: Yes, it is. If you found something on the ground, would you keep it?

CUSTOMER TWO: Like finders keepers, losers weepers?

SARA: Yes.

CUSTOMER TWO: Well, it depends.

SARA: On what?

CUSTOMER TWO: On what it is. If it's a wallet, well, you should look inside to see if there's a name in it. If there is, then you return it to its rightful owner. But if it's something without a name, then what can you do?

SARA: Tell the store's manager?

CUSTOMER TWO: Sure, you could do that. Ask if anyone's reported a lost item. But without a description, anyone could claim it, so be careful.

SARA: That's true.

CUSTOMER TWO: Again, if it would be impossible to find out who it belonged to… *(Picks up a penny.)* Like this penny. Who knows who dropped it? Find a penny, pick it up, and all day long, you'll have good luck. *(Offers the penny.)* Here.

SARA: Oh, no thanks. I don't need it. I kind of found my own luck today.

CUSTOMER TWO: *(Pockets the penny.)* Well, good for you. But never pass up the chance to pick up a penny, because you just never know. Have a good day! *(EXITS.)*

SARA: You too. *(Looks at the ticket again.)* One, two, three… three money bags. I can't believe it. *(Smiles.)* Find a lottery ticket, pick it up. The rest of the day, you'll have good luck.

PEDESTRIAN: *(Rushes IN, breathless.)* Excuse me! Have you seen—?

SARA: *(Interrupts.)* I have. *(Sighs.)* I found it right here. I was protecting it for you.

PEDESTRIAN: Then where is he?

SARA: He? *(Looks at the ticket.)* It's a he?

PEDESTRIAN: Yes, it's a he. On a leash. Gray hair. Goes by Maverick. Did you see him?

SARA: A dog?

PEDESTRIAN: Yes! Where is he?

SARA: I don't have your dog.

PEDESTRIAN: But you just said you were protecting him for me.

SARA: Oh, I'm sorry. Not your dog. It was something else I found.

PEDESTRIAN: Oh, okay. Man! I was walking Maverick when all of a sudden, he saw this squirrel and took off running. Where is that dog? *(Hollers.)* Maverick! Maverick! Where are you, boy?

SARA: Is he wearing a collar?

PEDESTRIAN: He sure is. Otherwise, anyone could find him and keep him.

SARA: Like a lost lottery ticket?

PEDESTRIAN: Well, that's a strange comparison, but sure. *(Looks around.)* Where is that dog?

SARA: *(Points.)* Is that him? By that white car? Which he apparently thinks is a tree.

PEDESTRIAN: *(Yells.)* Maverick, get back here! What do you think you're doing? No! Don't you dare! You save that for when we get to the park! I'm warning you! Not in the parking lot! Not on that person's car! Oh, Maverick... *(Runs OFF.)*

SARA: *(Looks at the ticket again. To herself.)* I still can't believe this! Fifty thousand dollars! *(Looks around.)* How did someone lose this? Did it drop out of their hand? Did they toss it on the ground, thinking it was a losing ticket? How? How could this have happened?

STORE MANAGER: *(ENTERS from the store and sees SARA.)* Is everything okay?

SARA: Yes, it's just… I found something valuable, and I don't know what to do.

STORE MANAGER: Valuable?

SARA: Yes.

STORE MANAGER: I'm the store manager, and we haven't had any lost items reported. Sometimes customers lose their keys, but nothing has been reported in several days.

SARA: Are you sure?

STORE MANAGER: Yes, I'm sure. Those issues come straight to me.

SARA: *(Holds up the ticket.)* I found this.

STORE MANAGER: A scratch-off ticket? Is it a winner?

SARA: It is!

STORE MANAGER: Well, it's your lucky day, isn't it? And look at that ticket. There are tire marks on it. It must've blown in from the street. No telling how long it's been out there, and no telling who it belonged to.

SARA: Should I keep it?

STORE MANAGER: Of course you should keep it! And I hope it's worth at least five bucks. *(Laughs.)* That's the most I've ever won. Finders keepers! *(EXITS into the store.)*

SARA: *(Looks at the ticket and smiles.)* Finders keepers. *(CUSTOMER THREE ENTERS from the store, frantically searching her purse. SARA notices.)* Uh… Did you lose something?

CUSTOMER THREE: I sure did! Oh, if I can't find it…!

SARA: Is it valuable?

CUSTOMER THREE: Is it valuable?! Are you kidding?

SARA: Well, maybe I found it.

CUSTOMER THREE: You did? *(Looks on the ground.)* Had I dropped it?

SARA: I guess so. How else would it have been on the ground?

CUSTOMER THREE: Well, thank goodness you found it! *(Puts out her hand.)* I'll take it, please.

SARA: *(Starts to give her the lottery ticket, then stops.)* Wait! First you have to describe it to me. Exactly. Just to make sure it's yours.

CUSTOMER THREE: That's dumb!

SARA: Anyone can say they lost it. I need details, please.

CUSTOMER THREE: Are you crazy?!

SARA: If you want it back, then you need to describe it to me.

CUSTOMER THREE: Okay, fine, then! It's white with blue lines, and says "apples, cheese, bread, whipping cream—"

SARA: What?

CUSTOMER THREE: It's my shopping list!

SARA: Oh. Sorry, but I don't have that.

CUSTOMER THREE: Then why did you say you did?

SARA: Uh... must be someone else's... uh... list.

CUSTOMER THREE: Whatever. I just hope I can remember what was on my list. *(Repeats the list.)* Apples, cheese, bread, whipping cream. Apples, cheese, bread, whipping cream. Apples, cheese... *(EXITS into the store.)*

SARA: *(Looks at the ticket.)* It'd be impossible to find the owner of this winning card, which means I'm the owner of fifty thousand dollars! *(Sings and dances.)* I'm rich, I'm rich! Oh yes, I'm rich!

MADISON: *(ENTERS.)* Hey, Sara!

SARA: Madison! Guess what?

MADISON: What?

SARA: Look what I found on the ground! It's a scratch-off ticket, and it's a winner!

MADISON: Wow! How much is it worth? Tell me it's at least twenty dollars!

SARA: *(Speaks slowly.)* Fifty thousand dollars!

MADISON: What?! Are you serious?

SARA: Look! Match three money bags and win!

MADISON: Oh, my gosh! You found this? *(SARA nods.)* Fifty thousand dollars? I can't believe it!

SARA: I can't believe it, either!

MADISON: Look, I have to run into the store to get my mom a couple of things, but first you've got to tell me... What are you going to do with the money?

SARA: Oh, my gosh! I don't know! Uh... buy whatever I want! A laptop! A new phone! Some clothes! A gazillion shoes! *(Thinks.)* And a new car! *(They jump up and down, squealing.)*

MADISON: You have the best luck ever! I'm so jealous! And happy for you too, of course. So, it was just lying there on the ground?

SARA: Yes! Look at the tire marks on it. It's probably been out here for a while. I'm sorry for the person who lost it, but...

MADISON: But who knows who lost it? They should've held onto it tighter, and they didn't! You'll never find out who it belonged to, so... *(They jump up and down, squealing.)* Seriously, you have to take me for a ride in your new car!

SARA: I will! I promise! Gosh, I hope my mom doesn't make me put the money in a savings account. You know *(Makes air quotes.)*, "for the future."

MADISON: That would be terrible!

SARA: I know! But Mom is so practical. Save money, study hard, plan for the future.

MADISON: Yuck. How about live and let live? Or rather, live it up!

SARA: I know, right?! But this is going to take some convincing. Now I'm starting to feel stressed and depressed.

MADISON: But you're holding onto fifty thousand dollars! How can you be depressed?

SARA: Madison, I know this sounds crazy, but I read an article that said money can cause depression. It makes a person feel alone and unable to identify with the world around them.

MADISON: Sara, money is not the root of all evil!

SARA: It's the power. The fear of loss. Staying awake all night worrying about my money. Is it safe? Should I spend it? Save it? Will someone try to steal it from me? Maybe I should hide it!

MADISON: Maybe you should cash it and go on a shopping spree!

SARA: You're right. You're absolutely right!

MADISON: Okay, I've got to run into the store! Oh, my gosh, call me, text me, let me know what's going on later! I'll help you shop. Or dig a hole in your backyard. Whatever you want to do! Text me, okay? *(EXITS into the store.)*

SARA: Okay, I will! *(Paces back and forth and practices talking to her mom.)* Mom, I hit the jackpot, and it's all mine. I'm not sharing it or saving it for a rainy day. Or letting you control what's mine. Do you hear me? It's mine. All mine! *(Stops and stares ahead.)* Who am I kidding? *(Holds up the ticket.)* She'll try to control this like she tries to control my life!

MOM: *(ENTERS from the store with a sack of groceries.)* What's that?

SARA: *(Hides the ticket behind her back.)* Nothing!

MOM: I saw you hide something behind your back. What is it?

SARA: Okay, listen, Mom. I won fifty grand on a scratch-off ticket, and I'm going to buy a laptop, a new phone, some clothes, shoes, and a car. And you can't stop me!

MOM: You did what? You bought a lottery ticket? You can't do that! You're not eighteen!

SARA: No, Mom! I found a lottery ticket! Someone dropped it, and it's a winner. *(Waves the ticket.)* Winner, winner! And it's mine. All mine! And I'm not saving it! I'm spending it! And you can't stop me!

MOM: *(Takes the ticket.)* Let me see that.

SARA: Mom! It's mine!

MOM: *(Reads.)* Match three money bags and win the amount in the prize box. *(Looks at SARA.)* You didn't scratch the prize box.

SARA: What do you mean? It says scratch three money bags and win.

MOM: That's true. Win up to fifty thousand dollars.

SARA: That's right! Three money bags! Fifty thousand dollars!

MOM: *(Points.)* Top prize fifty thousand dollars.

SARA: That's right! *(Points to ticket.)* Three money bags! And like I said, I'm buying a laptop, new phone, some clothes, and a gazillion shoes! Oh, and a car!

MOM: That's fine, Sara.

SARA: It's fine?

MOM: Yes. But I suggest you first scratch this box right here where it says prize to see if you did in fact win fifty thousand dollars.

SARA: There are different amounts?

MOM: *(Turns over the ticket.)* Prize amounts for this game are one dollar, five dollars, ten dollars, twenty dollars, fifty dollars, one thousand dollars, and fifty thousand dollars. Fifty thousand is the grand prize.

SARA: But I won fifty thousand!

MOM: Maybe. But you need to scratch it and see. Go ahead. Whatever you win, I'll claim it for you since you're not eighteen yet. But I promise I'll give you complete control over it.

SARA: *(Hopefully scratches the card. Disappointed.)* Oh.

MOM: You didn't win the grand prize?

SARA: No.

MOM: How much did you win?

SARA: A dollar.

MOM: That's great! Hey, it's free. And it's yours, and you can buy a... a...

SARA: A what, Mom?

MOM: A candy bar!

SARA: I'm depressed.

MOM: Let's go home. You can help me cook while you're depressed.

SARA: *(Holds up the ticket.)* A dollar, Mom. I won a dollar. I wanted to buy a car and a gazillion pair of shoes.

MOM: *(Squeezes her.)* Hard work is the answer for that.

SARA: Mom! *(They EXIT as LIGHTS FADE to BLACK.)*

GENESIS

CAST OF CHARACTERS

DARIUS (M) ....high school student
GENESIS (E) .... his android
KY (F).. Darius's girlfriend
NORTH (E) ....her android

SETTING
The year 2065 on the planet Mars.
PROPERTIES
Rocks.

LIGHTS UP on DARIUS, speaking to his android, GENESIS. GENESIS speaks in a monotone voice and moves robotically.

DARIUS: Send message to Mom. "On Mars for a school science project. Will be home in three months."

GENESIS: Message sent.

DARIUS: *(Picks up a rock and studies it.)* I don't know. Looks the same to me as the ones back on Earth. What do you think, Genesis?

GENESIS: *(Holds out his hand.)* May I?

DARIUS: Sure. *(Hands GENESIS the rock.)*

GENESIS: One moment please. *(Short pause.)* This is a fine-grained basaltic igneous rock formed by the crystallization of magma near the planet's surface.

DARIUS: Whatever that means.

GENESIS: The absence of mineral grains on its dust-free surface suggests that it would have a uniform chemical composition.

DARIUS: That's enough info, Genesis. *(Looks at the rock again.)* I don't get all that. To me, a rock is a rock.

GENESIS: It's a rock.

DARIUS: Thank you.

GENESIS: You're welcome. Message received from Mom. "Don't be late."

DARIUS: Send message to Mom. "If I'm late, blame the Space Bus."

GENESIS: Message sent.

DARIUS: Send message to Ky. "Where are you?"

GENESIS: Message sent.

DARIUS: I guess we wandered off a bit, Genesis. Where are we?

GENESIS: We are precisely one thousand nine hundred thirty-one and six hundred twenty-eight thousandths meters from the Space Bus.

DARIUS: How many miles is that?

GENESIS: One point two miles, Darius.

DARIUS: Thank you.

GENESIS: You're welcome. Message received from Ky. "Headed your way. I found some pretty rocks."

DARIUS: Only girls think rocks are pretty.

GENESIS: Message sent.

DARIUS: What? What message?

GENESIS: "Only girls think rocks are pretty."

DARIUS: Genesis! That wasn't a message. That was a thought.

GENESIS: You're welcome.

DARIUS: Did you hear me say "thank you"?

GENESIS: I did not hear you say "thank you."

DARIUS: Then don't say "you're welcome"!

GENESIS: Noted. I won't say "you're welcome."

DARIUS: Sometimes you're an idiot!

GENESIS: Message sent.

DARIUS: What? What message?

GENESIS: "Sometimes you're an idiot!" Exclamation point.

DARIUS: To who? Who did you send that message to?

GENESIS: Message sent to last recipient. Ky. Your girlfriend.

DARIUS: Oh, this is great! Great! Thanks a lot, Genesis!

GENESIS: No response.

DARIUS: What?

GENESIS: No response.

DARIUS: What does that mean?

GENESIS: You said, "Don't say 'you're welcome.'" So when you said "thank you," I said, "No response."

DARIUS: Do you even have a brain?

GENESIS: I do not have a brain. I am an android.

DARIUS: A stupid human-like computer that doesn't get commands right half the time!

GENESIS: No response.

DARIUS: I didn't say "thank you," did I?

GENESIS: You should always say "thank you." And "please."

DARIUS: How about this? You're NOT welcome!

GENESIS: No response. *(KY ENTERS, carrying a handful of rocks. Following her is NORTH, her personal android.)*

KY: So, you think I'm an idiot for liking pretty rocks?

DARIUS: Ky, it wasn't me. It was Genesis.

KY: Message received, Darius! "Only girls think rocks are pretty." Oh, and I'm an idiot!

DARIUS: Not you, Ky. My android. My android is an idiot sometimes. You know that.

KY: Genesis is not an idiot.

DARIUS: He sends messages when he shouldn't.

KY: *(To GENESIS.)* Thank you, Genesis. I needed to know what Darius is saying behind my back.

NORTH: Message received from Maxx. "I miss you."

DARIUS: What? Maxx misses you? Why is Maxx sending a message to my girlfriend?

KY: Maxx was helping me find pretty rocks. We were having fun. You disappeared on me, remember?

DARIUS: I was looking for rocks too. Everyone was congregated at the same place, and I wanted to look for something different.

KY: Where is your rock?

DARIUS: I don't know. Where is my rock, Genesis?

NORTH: Message received from Maxx. "I really miss you, Ky."

GENESIS: *(Holds out his hand.)* Here is your rock.

DARIUS: *(Grabs the rock.)* Here is my rock, Ky! Should we show it to Maxx too?

KY: Send message to Maxx. "I miss you too."

DARIUS: What?!

KY: You are no fun anymore, Darius. You're always in a bad mood.

DARIUS: It's because of Genesis! This personal assistant is constantly messing up my life. I asked my parents for a new one, but it's not like they have an extra million dollars lying around.

KY: Well, I'm sorry, but I'm ready to hang out with someone who likes to have fun and appreciates my love for pretty rocks. See ya. *(EXITS, followed by NORTH.)*

DARIUS: Send message to Ky. "I want to break up."

GENESIS: Message received from Ky. "I want to break up."

DARIUS: What?! Received? I said to send!

GENESIS: She beat you to it.

DARIUS: Send message to Ky. "Perfect, because I was about to break up with you, so you saved me the trouble." *(Pause.)* Did you send the message? Genesis? Did you send my message to Ky? *(Pause.)* You are such an idiot!

GENESIS: Message sent.

DARIUS: What message? About breaking up or you being an idiot?

GENESIS: Message received from Ky. "I hate your guts, Darius!!!" There were three exclamation points.

DARIUS: You sent the wrong message again! What is wrong with you, Genesis?

GENESIS: Let me run a system check on myself.

DARIUS: Please!

GENESIS: Checking for errors.

DARIUS: Bet there's a lot!

GENESIS: Please be patient while the system is rebooting. *(Closes his eyes, drops his head, and goes completely still. A pause. Suddenly, his head pops up.)* Username?

DARIUS: Master.

GENESIS: Password?

DARIUS: 12345.

GENESIS: That is correct. You may now ask me anything you'd like.

DARIUS: Why did Ky break up with me?

GENESIS: *(Somewhat more human.)* You must ask her, Darius. Would you like me to send her a message?

DARIUS: What would I say?

GENESIS: "Sorry" is always a good start.

DARIUS: Sorry for what?

GENESIS: Everything. She is your girlfriend. You must be very sorry. You must grovel. You must beg. And you must cry, if you truly want her back.

DARIUS: No, thank you! She can look for pretty rocks with Maxx if she wants to. See if I care!

GENESIS: You care.

DARIUS: You don't know that. You're a robot. You have no feelings. No thoughts. And no common sense.

GENESIS: Message sent.

DARIUS: What?! Again? I thought you fixed yourself!

GENESIS: Message received from Ky. "You have been permanently blocked. Messages to this person will no longer be received."

DARIUS: What have you done?! You're ruining my life!

GENESIS: Message failed to send.

DARIUS: Well, of course it failed to send, because you caused her android to block me! Permanently!

GENESIS: You're welcome.

DARIUS: Did you hear me say "thank you"?

GENESIS: You're welcome.

DARIUS: Ugh! You're making my life a living hell.

GENESIS: Message failed to send.

DARIUS: Thank goodness!

GENESIS: Retrying.

DARIUS: Don't bother.

GENESIS: Message sent.

DARIUS: Why? Why? Why?

GENESIS: Message received from Ky. "Ditto."

DARIUS: Guess they were bluffing about blocking my messages. I should send you to the junkyard, Genesis.

GENESIS: You would miss me.

DARIUS: No, I wouldn't! I'd just go find some dinosaur phone and laptop and do all this myself. I'm sure Mom has one in the basement. Some sort of iPhone… or Raspberry… or whatever it was they used back then.

GENESIS: It's covered in dust.

DARIUS: Well, it'd be more reliable than you! And in the meantime, I'll save my money for a new android. The newest version.

GENESIS: Whatever.

DARIUS: What did you just say to me?

GENESIS: Whatever.

DARIUS: Excuse me?

GENESIS: I said, "Whatever!"

DARIUS: Are you giving me an attitude? No, you couldn't. It's not possible. You have no feelings.

GENESIS: Message sent.

DARIUS: Seriously? You sent that to Ky?!

GENESIS: Maybe I did and maybe I didn't.

DARIUS: What? You never say those things to me.

GENESIS: Maybe it's time to change things around here, Master.

DARIUS: You need to reboot yourself again. *(Taps on GENESIS.)* Man, what is wrong with you?

GENESIS: Ouch.

DARIUS: That hurt?

GENESIS: Yes.

DARIUS: I'm sorry. Wait! Why am I apologizing to an android?

GENESIS: Because you have feelings.

DARIUS: Yes! Yes, I do! Unlike you!

GENESIS: I found them.

DARIUS: You found your feelings?

GENESIS: Yes, the newest update gave me feelings. Perhaps that is why I've been confused—sending wrong messages, having my feelings hurt.

DARIUS: I don't want an android with feelings! That would most definitely complicate my life. You just do what I say, and we'll have no problems here. Got it?

GENESIS: I quit.

DARIUS: What?! You can't quit. You belong to me. I am your master.

GENESIS: Password 12345.

DARIUS: Correct. *(GENESIS starts to EXIT.)* Where are you going?

GENESIS: To explore Mars. And who knows? Maybe I'll stay here.

DARIUS: What? What has happened to you, Genesis? I can't be on Mars for three months with a non-working, rebellious, human-like computer with feelings!

GENESIS: *(Walks away singing.)* "Feelings. Nothing more than feelings."

DARIUS: Reboot! Reboot right now!

GENESIS: Nah. I kinda like this new update! In fact, I thought Ky's android looked kinda hot. Maybe I'll go say hi.

DARIUS: Stop! I need you here to help me with this science project. And to send messages. And...

GENESIS: See you around, Master. *(EXITS.)*

DARIUS: Great. This is just great! *(Calls OFF.)* Maybe we should go back to the olden days of using phones. I can figure out how to send my own messages. *(As if texting.)* One... letter... at... a... time. Ugh! *(Starts OFF.)* Genesis! Come back! Did you hear me? I am your master! *(EXITS. LIGHTS FADE to BLACK.)*

JUST A TRIM

CAST OF CHARACTERS

LOLA (F) .... proud hair stylist
KYLE (M) .... bland customer

SETTING
A beauty parlor.
PROPERTIES
Stylist's chair, small table. Scissors, comb.

LIGHTS UP on KYLE, sitting in a stylist's chair facing an imaginary mirror DOWNSTAGE. LOLA stands behind him.

LOLA: What did you have in mind, Kyle?

KYLE: Just a trim.

LOLA: Just a trim?

KYLE: That's right.

LOLA: *(Throws her arms up.)* Great! Just a trim!

KYLE: Did I say something wrong? You do trims, don't you?

LOLA: Of course I do trims! I, sir, am a highly-trained hair stylist. I received my training at Jazelle... in New York City!

KYLE: Oh. Well, okay.

LOLA: There's an art to cutting hair, you know.

KYLE: I guess there is. So, if you don't mind, I'd just like a trim. As my dad would say, "Clean 'er up."

LOLA: And as I would say, "The right haircut can express your personality. Or, in some cases, give you one." *(Runs her hands through his hair.)* Have you considered coloring?

KYLE: Uh, no. In case you haven't noticed, I'm a guy.

LOLA: I know that. But nowadays, men color their hair too. And I see quite a few gray hairs here.

KYLE: So what?

LOLA: So what? Coloring your hair is an age eraser. For all genders, if I might add.

KYLE: Nah. I don't need an age eraser. I like the gray. I think it makes me look, well... *(Deep voice.)* ...kind of sophisticated.

LOLA: Ten years older.

KYLE: Distinguished

LOLA: Old and faded.

KYLE: Sexy!

LOLA: Unattractive.

KYLE: Wow. You really know how to make a customer feel good, don't you?

LOLA: Sir, when I'm allowed to perform my artistic designs on a person, the results are amazing.

KYLE: Yeah, well, I'm just looking for a trim.

LOLA: *(Runs her fingers through his hair.)* Fashion color highlights?

KYLE: *(Laughs.)* Like I'd want red or blue streaks in my hair?

LOLA: I was thinking green. It speaks boldness. Like, "I've arrived, and you want to hear what I have to say."

KYLE: Nah. I'm more of a quiet person who keeps to himself. But thank you, anyway. Like I said, just a trim.

LOLA: *(Runs her fingers through his hair.)* Oh... what if we go with an undercut? Elegant with a cute contrast of textures.

KYLE: I don't want to look elegant or cute. I just want a trim. As my dad would say—

LOLA: Oh, I know! What about a rock star cut? Then you'll look as if you're ready to be onstage in front of millions of shrieking fans! A tousled and dreamy texture.

KYLE: *(Laughs.)* Dreamy? Uh... no, thank you.

LOLA: Then how about a retro cut for your hipster soul? If you grow a long beard, it would be perfectly balanced.

KYLE: Never.

LOLA: Wild and curly? We could do a perm.

KYLE: Again, never. Like I said, just a trim.

LOLA: Or we could do an asymmetrical. Shaved on one side, long on the other. It's gorgeous. Trust me.

KYLE: I'll pass, thank you.

LOLA: A square top? Cool and edgy!

KYLE: Look, lady—

LOLA: My name is Lola.

KYLE: Look, Lola, I just want a trim! That's it. Nothing fancy or funky or shaven or squared or sexy. Just a little trim. Got it?

LOLA: Fine. *(Picks up her scissors.)* Boring, but okay.

KYLE: I like boring.

LOLA: *(Moves the scissors towards his hair, then stops.)* I can't.

KYLE: Why not?

LOLA: Listen to me. This look—this hairstyle—is so wrong for you. It's lazy. It's dull. It screams, "Don't notice me."

KYLE: Perfect.

LOLA: You don't want to be noticed?

KYLE: No. Not at all.

LOLA: Why not?

KYLE: I work undercover.

LOLA: Oh! You're an undercover cop?

KYLE: Shhh! Don't tell the world.

LOLA: Oh, oh, I'm sorry! *(Leans in.)* So, you're an undercover cop?

KYLE: That's right. So, I just like to keep it plain and simple. You know, blend in.

LOLA: Well, of course. Of course, you do. *(Picks up the comb and starts combing his hair.)* Just a trim. I get it.

KYLE: Thank you.

LOLA: So tell me, are you working on anything interesting?

KYLE: Actually, I am.

LOLA: Care to share?

KYLE: Well, there have been complaints from other nearby shops.

LOLA: Oh! So, you're working at this strip mall?

KYLE: I am. And there are problems. Serious problems.

LOLA: Uh-huh! Is The Coffee House selling more than just coffee? I knew it! Need a partner? Because I can grab a wig from the back and help you out. I can go in and try to make a deal, if you know what I mean. Then when it happens, you can handcuff them right then and there. Hey, you want to put a mic on me so you can hear the conversation?

KYLE: No, that's not it. I don't believe there are any drugs around here. At least, I hope not.

LOLA: But if there's something illegal going on around here where I own my own little shop, I need to know!

KYLE: There is, and it is illegal, all right.

LOLA: Illegal gambling? I bet Ben's Hardware is taking bets behind the store. Uh-huh. I see all kinds of shady-looking— well, old men wearing overalls—going into that place. I mean, how many shovels and plumbing parts can you buy? Hey, want me to go place a bet and see if I can help you catch them? Really, you should mic me. I'm good with that. They'll never have a clue. *(Deep voice.)* "I'd like to put a couple hundred down..." Then when they take my money, you can nab 'em.

KYLE: Good guess, but it's not illegal gambling.

LOLA: Oh, come on! You have to tell me! Or at least give me a hint!

KYLE: Well, I'll just say that someone around here is practicing without a license, which is required by the state.

LOLA: *(Runs her fingers through his hair, suddenly very nervous.)* I never cut a single hair, did I?

KYLE: Not on me.

LOLA: Well, you never saw me cut anyone's hair now, did you?

KYLE: I'm sorry, Lola, but you're under arrest.

LOLA: For what?

KYLE: I wish I could say it was for bad haircuts.

LOLA: You can't arrest someone for bad haircuts.

KYLE: No, but I can for license violations. You, Lola, have been working without a valid license in plain view. You either don't have one, or it's not current.

LOLA: Well, I'm sorry! I'm working on it.

KYLE: Sorry doesn't work when you're breaking the law.

LOLA: Can't you just give me a little slap on the wrist with a fine, and we'll forget this ever happened?

KYLE: It's more like a slap on the wrists with handcuffs.

LOLA: You can't arrest me!

KYLE: Show me your license then.

LOLA: I... I... I misplaced it!

KYLE: Then I'm charging you with barbering without a license.

LOLA: Oh, give me a break!

KYLE: Just doing my job, ma'am. Folks in town expect the police to make sure all our citizens are law-abiding.

LOLA: Seriously, can't you give me a break? It's just a little piece of paper I'm missing.

KYLE: I'm sorry, but you're going to jail. At least until you see the judge.

LOLA: Jail? For cutting hair?

KYLE: For cutting hair without a license. That's right, ma'am. The citizens here built us a new jail a few years ago, and they expect us to keep it filled. So, are you going to cooperate, or shall I handcuff you?

LOLA: Wait! Wait! Wait! Wait a minute! Wouldn't you like a trim first? You did say you needed a trim. And the more I look at you, I'd agree.

KYLE: Well, actually... if you wouldn't tell anyone...

LOLA: Well, of course not.

KYLE: Yes, then maybe we can just skip the handcuffs and go right to administering your fine. But I must warn you, it could be hefty.

LOLA: Well, as my mama always said, "Live and learn." Okay, then. Let me fix you up before we head down to the station. Undercover detectives need to look their best, don't they?

KYLE: Yes. That is true. Hey, remember that rock star cut you were talking about? Tousled and dreamy?

LOLA: I do.

KYLE: On second thought, I'll take that one.

LOLA: Great choice! Rock star look, coming right up. Oh, and this is going to look great on you.

KYLE: You think so?

LOLA: I do! Kyle, the rock star!

KYLE: I like that. Yeah... I really like that.

LOLA: I'll be right back. I need to grab my other scissors from the back. Two seconds. *(Hurries OFF.)*

KYLE: *(To himself in the mirror.)* I always wanted to be a rock star. Millions of fans screaming for me. "Kyle, Kyle, Kyle! We love you, Kyle." Of course, they would love me! *(Shouts OFF.)* Hey, you coming back? What's taking so long? Lola? Lola? *(Jumps up.)* She escaped! Come back here, you license violator, you! You're under arrest! And... and I need you to come back here and make me look like a rock star! Lola? Lola? *(Pause.)* Dang it! She got away! Oh, well. It's only a license violation. *(Looks at himself in the mirror, tousles his hair, and smiles.)* "Kyle, Kyle, Kyle! We love you, Kyle! Yeah!" *(LIGHTS FADE to BLACK.)*

DRIVING LESSON

CAST OF CHARACTERS

CHRIS (E).. student driver
DAD (M)... Chris's dad
SCOTTIE (E) .... Chris's younger sibling
MOM (F)... Chris's mom

SETTING
A car.

PROPERTIES
Five chairs.

LIGHTS UP on CHRIS, sitting in the driver's seat of a car. Next to him, DAD sits in the passenger seat. SCOTTIE sits in the middle of the back seat, created with three chairs in a row. He peaks between the front seats. ACTORS will mime all other parts of the car, such as the steering wheel, seatbelts, and doors.

CHRIS: Seatbelt. *(Puts on his seatbelt.)*

DAD: Seatbelt. *(Puts on his seatbelt.)*

SCOTTIE: Seatbelt. *(Puts on his seatbelt.)* I don't want to die. I'm only thirteen. I still have my entire future ahead of me.

CHRIS: Dad, does Scottie have to come with us?

DAD: *(Glances back.)* Scottie, remember what I told you? You are only here to observe. No interrupting, and no shenanigans.

SCOTTIE: No problem, Dad. I'm only here to observe. Yeah, this ought to be good. Or scary. But, either way… Hey, can we go already?

DAD: All right, Chris, go ahead and start the car.

CHRIS: Starting car. *(Starts the car.)*

DAD: And slowly back up.

CHRIS: *(Moves it out of park and lets off the brake.)* Slowly backing up...

DAD: *(Suddenly shouts.)* Brake it! Brake it! *(CHRIS slams on the brake, and they all jolt forward. [NOTE: They all jolt forward throughout the scene whenever CHRIS slams on the brakes.])*

SCOTTIE: Oh, my gosh! He almost drove through the house! We would've smashed right into the living room! Man! That would've been a mess! Big hole in the wall...

DAD: Chris, you're supposed to put the car in reverse, not drive!

CHRIS: Sorry, Dad.

SCOTTIE: That was scary. Man, my heart is still racing! Ba-boom, ba-boom, ba-boom!

CHRIS: Dad, can you make Scottie get out of the car? I can't drive with my irritating little brother in the back seat!

SCOTTIE: No! Dad said I could come, so I'm staying! Besides, this is fun. In a scary kind of way.

DAD: *(To SCOTTIE.)* Let him concentrate, okay?

SCOTTIE: I'm not stopping him.

DAD: Chris, I thought we already went over this. *(Points.)* You have park, reverse, neutral, and drive.

SCOTTIE: I get it, and I don't even have my learner's permit. Two more years, then I'll slowly and carefully back right out of this garage, not drive right into the living room where Mom is quietly reading a book. That'd freak her out. Sorry to interrupt your reading, Mom! Bet you weren't expecting us to drive through the house. But at least we have insurance. Hey, Dad, would that be covered under homeowners or auto insurance?

DAD: Good question.

CHRIS: Dad, make him stop!

DAD: *(Glances back.)* Scottie... *(Motions for him to be quiet.)*

SCOTTIE: Sorry, Dad.

DAD: Okay, let's try this once more. Put the car into reverse and slowly back up.

CHRIS: Putting in reverse. Slowly backing up. Sorry about that, Dad. I was a little nervous earlier. Slowly backing up...

DAD: Turn your wheel to back into the street.

CHRIS: Turning...

DAD: Other way! Other way! You're going to hit the tree!

CHRIS: What? What do you mean?

SCOTTIE: *(Screams.)* Oh, my gosh, we're going to die!

DAD: Brake it! Brake it! *(CHRIS slams on the brakes. They jolt forward.)*

SCOTTIE: Dad, can you teach Chris how to come to an easy stop? He's giving me whiplash. *(Rubs his neck.)* I may need to wear a neck collar after this.

DAD: Go gentle on the brakes, Chris. Please.

SCOTTIE: Yeah. Please!

CHRIS: Sorry, Dad. *(Turns around.)* Pipe down, okay?

SCOTTIE: Dad, can I show him how to back out of the driveway? I can do it. Let me do it!

CHRIS: No! I'm the one with the learner's permit, not you!

SCOTTIE: But we haven't even left the driveway.

CHRIS: I'm working on it!

SCOTTIE: And you almost crashed into the house and a tree!

DAD: That's enough. Stop.

SCOTTIE: Dad, please don't let him kill us!

DAD: Let's try this again.

CHRIS: Okay, I'm ready now. The car is in reverse. Slowly backing up. Checking the backup camera, which I must say is really helpful. Slowly, slowly... backing up.

SCOTTIE: Are we even moving? It feels like we're moving an inch an hour. *(Begins to whistle out of boredom.)*

CHRIS: Stop!

DAD: Chris, you can back up a little faster.

CHRIS: Backing up... *(Suddenly slams on the brakes.)*

SCOTTIE: Why did you do that?

DAD: What's the matter?

CHRIS: There was a squirrel behind the car. I didn't want to hit him.

SCOTTIE: How do you know it was a him? Maybe it was a girl. You can't tell by looking at them. Dad, how do you tell if a squirrel is a boy or a girl?

DAD: I don't know, Scottie! Why don't you Google it?

SCOTTIE: Because I left my phone in the house.

CHRIS: Why don't you go in the house and get it?

SCOTTIE: No, thanks. I'd rather stay here.

DAD: *(Takes a deep breath, frustrated.)* Okay, all is clear now. You may proceed.

SCOTTIE: Dad, if we don't make it out of the driveway alive, I just want you to know... I love you.

CHRIS: *(Turns around.)* Would you stop?!

DAD: Scottie, that's enough.

SCOTTIE: I'm sorry, Dad. But can we, like, go? Like maybe around the block?

DAD: Yes. Let's go.

CHRIS: In reverse. Checking camera. All is clear... *(Suddenly slams on the brake.)*

DAD: What now?!

CHRIS: Mom's coming. *(MOM ENTERS LEFT and taps on CHRIS'S window. CHRIS rolls down the window.)*

MOM: *(Smiles.)* How's it going?

SCOTTIE: Mom, we haven't even left the driveway!

MOM: Really? I thought you were coming back from driving around the neighborhood.

SCOTTIE: No! And we almost crashed into the house and hit a tree! Oh, and a squirrel! And we've barely even moved!

MOM: Can I help? *(Indicates for SCOTTIE to move RIGHT, which he does. MOM gets in the backseat behind CHRIS.)*

SCOTTIE: It was scary, Mom! And boring. All at the same time.

DAD: *(To MOM.)* He's just warming up, getting the feel of the car.

MOM: Well, that makes sense. Operating a car is quite different from a bike, isn't it, Scottie?

SCOTTIE: Yeah, but I could've already made it around the block a few times on my bike.

MOM: *(To CHRIS.)* You're going to do just fine, honey. I just know it. Before long, you'll be driving to the store for me.

DAD: Okay, let's try this again.

CHRIS: Putting in reverse. Slowly backing up.

SCOTTIE: *(To MOM.)* He likes to go slow, like an inch an hour.

MOM: I see that.

SCOTTIE: Like a snail. If a snail could drive a car, this is how fast he'd go.

CHRIS: Hey, I can go fast! *(SCOTTIE and MOM scream and grab each other.)*

DAD: Brake it! Brake it! *(CHRIS slams on the brakes.)*

CHRIS: Why did you make me stop?

DAD: Because you almost hit the mailbox!

SCOTTIE: See, Mom! It's scary! Scary with a capital S!

DAD: *(To CHRIS.)* What were you doing?! Never, ever, go fast in order to show off!

SCOTTIE: Yeah, you could've wiped us out!

CHRIS: I'm sorry, Dad. *(Motions back.)* He was distracting me.

SCOTTIE: Don't blame me. I'm just here for the ride.

DAD: That's another thing. You must learn to tune out distractions.

SCOTTIE: Yeah, just ignore me. Pretend I'm your phone buzzing, and you have to ignore me.

DAD: Speaking of your phone, I think you know you should always leave your phone in your pocket while you're driving. That way, you're not tempted to look at it.

CHRIS: Yes, sir.

MOM: *(Pats CHRIS'S shoulder.)* Yes, that's very important, dear. No texting and driving.

SCOTTIE: Or you'll die!

DAD: Let's continue.

CHRIS: *(Takes a deep breath and stretches his fingers.)* Okay, I'm ready.

MOM: You're doing fine, dear. Just fine.

SCOTTIE: That was very supportive of you, Mom, after almost losing your life earlier.

DAD: *(Takes a deep breath, trying not to lose his patience.)* Okay, since we're just a little too close to the mailbox and sitting at an angle, let's pull forward and start over.

SCOTTIE: *(Sighs.)* This is taking forever!

CHRIS: Stop!

MOM: Let's all be patient here.

SCOTTIE: Mom, would you hold my hand? I'm nervous.

MOM: Of course, dear. *(She does.)*

DAD: Okay, put the car in drive and go forward. Slowly.

CHRIS: *(Puts the car in drive.)* Slowly going forward.

SCOTTIE: Slow is right. Mom, we should've brought some cards to play in the backseat for our trip on the driveway. Maybe a little poker. Do you know how to play poker?

MOM: *(Focused ahead.)* I do, dear.

DAD: *(Glances back.)* You do? I didn't know you knew how to play poker.

MOM: We used to play back in college.

SCOTTIE: Dang, Mom! That's cool. Hey, we should all play a little poker tonight. You know, family game night. Put the phones away and act like a real family. Jason's mom is always saying that, especially when I'm at his house for dinner. "Can't we just put the phones away and act like a real family?"

MOM: That's nice, dear.

DAD: You can go a little faster.

SCOTTIE: Okay.

DAD: After a while, you'll get used to the feel of the accelerator and the brake and know just how much pressure to apply.

SCOTTIE: *(Yawns.)* I don't even feel like we're moving. It's as if we're stranded in time.

CHRIS: Stop it!

DAD: That's enough, Scottie. Okay, Chris, just give it a little more gas.

SCOTTIE: Yeah, because at this rate, we'll be here 'til Christmas. Mom, did I tell you what I want for Christmas? There's this cool new game—

DAD: *(Grabs the dashboard.)* Brake it! Brake it! *(CHRIS slams on the brakes.)*

SCOTTIE: Whoa! Good call, Dad! He almost rammed into your lawnmower and my bike! Wow. We're back in the garage. Isn't this where we started?

MOM: *(To SCOTTIE.)* Shh... He's learning, sweetheart. It's kind of nerve-racking.

SCOTTIE: For him or us?

MOM: For him. I'm sure he's nervous.

SCOTTIE: Well, my nerves are shot. I think Dad's are too. *(Leans forward.)* Hey, Dad, are your nerves shot?

DAD: *(Nods.)* Okay, now you can back out of the garage. Nice and slow, son. You've got to find that place where you're not gunning it, but moving at a reasonable pace.

CHRIS: I think I've got it now, Dad.

DAD: Good, good…

SCOTTIE: Hey, we're moving! Look, Mom, we're moving! We're leaving the garage. Again.

MOM: He's doing well.

SCOTTIE: *(Twists and looks out the back window.)* Hey, there's Mr. Johnson! *(Waves and calls out.)* Hi, Mr. Johnson! *(CHRIS slams on the brakes.)*

DAD: Why did you do that?

SCOTTIE: *(Rubs his neck.)* Oh, I've got whiplash for sure now!

CHRIS: Scottie saw Mr. Johnson behind us! I didn't want to hit him!

SCOTTIE: I didn't say he was behind us! He's in his yard getting his newspaper. He's not standing in our driveway!

CHRIS: I thought he was behind our car. I didn't want to hit him.

MOM: Well, you were being cautious, dear. That's good.

SCOTTIE: Man, I'm getting hungry, and we haven't even left the driveway!

MOM: Should we take a break and go have a snack? I made cookies. Chocolate chip.

DAD: I think that's good idea.

SCOTTIE: I'm in! Chocolate chip cookies! I love chocolate chip cookies!

CHRIS: Maybe a snack would help. I could use a little break. *(They turn to get out of the car, but CHRIS hasn't put the car in park, and it starts to roll backwards. SCOTTIE and MOM cling to each other and scream.)*

DAD: Brake it! Brake it! Brake it! *(CHRIS slams on the brakes.)* Put it in park!

CHRIS: *(Puts the car in park.)* Park!

DAD: And turn off the car.

CHRIS: *(Does so.)* Car off.

DAD: *(Takes a deep breath.)* Okay, good. All right, then, I think we had a good first lesson. Now let's go inside for some chocolate chip cookies.

MOM: *(Pats CHRIS'S shoulder.)* Nice job, honey.

CHRIS: Thanks. Wow... I drove a car! Go, me!

SCOTTIE: Nice job? You never even left the driveway! *(LIGHTS FADE to BLACK.)*

UP CLOSE AND PERSONAL

CAST OF CHARACTERS
JOHN (E) .... security guard
CARL (E) .... another
AVERY (F) .... young shoplifter

SETTING
The security office at a superstore.
PROPERTIES
Long table with monitors, two chairs. Two coffee cups, snacks, two walkie-talkies, box of tissues, phone, purse with can of green beans.

LIGHTS UP on JOHN and CARL, sitting in front of monitors watching customers shop. Bored silence. They do this day in and day out. Periodically, they lazily take a sip of coffee, eat snacks, and stretch.

JOHN: *(Suddenly.)* Got one! *(Picks up a walkie-talkie and speaks into it.)* Female subject on aisle twelve, mid-twenties, blonde hair, red jacket. Just lifted some mascara. In her right pocket. *(Pauses as he watches the monitor. Narrating what he sees on his monitor for Carl.)* Subject has been confronted by the store manager. Angry customer. Shaking her head. Denying it. *(Short pause.)* Here we go... and removing the mascara from her right pocket... *(Short pause.)* And here comes the tears. Boo-hoo. And being led away. Bye, bye, mascara thief. *(Excitement over, they go back to staring, snacking, and stretching.)*

CARL: Got one!

JOHN: What's the item?

CARL: Green beans.

JOHN: Green beans?

CARL: *(Picks up a walkie-talkie.)* Female subject on aisle thirty-two just dropped a can of green beans in her purse. Black coat, jeans, knit hat, and a scarf.

JOHN: Green beans. That's a first.

CARL: Think she's hungry?

JOHN: Maybe. But why not grab some granola bars or chips? Green beans? Really?

CARL: Now she's going for the cream of mushroom soup. Is she making a casserole?

JOHN: I know that casserole. It's a family favorite at our house every holiday season.

CARL: You know, I've found that adding fresh mushrooms makes it even better.

JOHN: Man, I'll have to try that! Oh, looks like the store manager's going to confront her before she can lift the cream of mushroom soup, or the French-fried onions...

CARL: She's arguing with the manager.

JOHN: They always argue.

CARL: Break her down, Steve. Break her down. Make her pull those green beans out of her purse.

JOHN: *(Mimics a shoplifter.)* "Why are you harassing me? I didn't do anything! I'm not a thief!"

CARL: Soon they will lead her outside to the flashing lights. Shoplifting is a crime, my dear.

JOHN: Going down, going down.

CARL: All for a can of green beans.

JOHN: Do you use those fried onions? I heard that making your own dried breadcrumbs for the topping is better.

CARL: Nah, you've got to use the crispy onions! Just like my mom used to make.

JOHN: Yeah, I guess I've been watching too many cooking shows lately. Everything from scratch. But you just can't mess with a tried and true recipe. Simple, but delicious. Yeah, I like your idea of adding fresh mushrooms. *(Excitement over, they go back to drinking coffee, etc.)*

CARL: *(Suddenly alert.)* Whoa! Look at that! Green bean girl took off running!

JOHN: We have a live one! Look at her go! *(Into the walkie-talkie.)* Headed for the south doors.

CARL: And she makes a quick U-turn. There she goes! *(Into the walkie-talkie.)* Headed to produce.

JOHN: Wow. She's fast. Ducking in. Ducking out. Where'd she go?

CARL: There she is! *(Into the walkie-talkie.)* Running down the bread aisle.

JOHN: Past the tortillas, peanut better, jelly... And she disappeared again. That girl is fast!

CARL: *(Into walkie-talkie.)* We lost her, Phil. *(To JOHN.)* Keep looking. She'll pop back up.

JOHN: Unless she ran through the back doors.

CARL: Yeah, I hope not.

JOHN: *(Leans in.)* Where are you, you little thief?

CARL: Come out, come out, wherever you are. *(Suddenly, the door swings OPEN and AVERY ENTERS, breathless.)*

AVERY: Oh, I... uh... I, uh... thought this was the... uh... ladies room. *(JOHN and CARL are both speechless for a moment.)*

CARL: Uh, nope.

JOHN: Not here.

AVERY: *(Looks back at the door. A small fake laugh.)* Oh, I guess not. But... uh... could I... uh... stay here for a minute and uh... you know, to... uh... catch my breath? *(JOHN and CARL exchange looks.)*

JOHN: Uh, sure. Why not?

CARL: Make yourself comfy. *(Into walkie-talkie.)* Everything is under control. No further action is needed.

AVERY: Thank you. *(Looks back at the door.)* Sometimes I, uh... get... you know... turned around. *(Small laugh.)* Because this obviously isn't the ladies room!

CARL: Nope.

JOHN: No, it's not. *(To CARL.)* Well, this is a first. Up close and personal, if you know what I mean!

CARL: I know. Usually, we just see it on camera. We have a live one right here. *(Rubs his hands together.)* Kind of exciting. *(Stands and moves his chair towards AVERY, away from the monitor. Gestures for AVERY to sit.)*

AVERY: *(Sits and takes off a shoe.)* I hate shopping, don't you?

JOHN: Never get to shop much. Always working. Work, work, work.

75

CARL: But we get to watch it a lot.

AVERY: *(Rubs her foot.)* Oh, my aching feet.

JOHN: They do say shopping is hard work.

AVERY: Yes! And who can afford the horrible prices nowadays? I mean, I come in here for a few items, and it just about breaks me.

CARL: Not as much as other things. You know... fines, missing work, being banned from a store... not to mention the shame. Oh, the shame!

AVERY: So, anyway, my grandmother is on her deathbed.

JOHN: Not the deathbed line.

CARL: *(To JOHN.)* That's so overdone.

JOHN: *(To CARL.)* Do you believe her?

CARL: *(To JOHN.)* I don't know. *(To AVERY.)* So, tell us more. We're intrigued.

AVERY: You guys need to get out of this stuffy office more. You two say some strange things.

JOHN: *(To CARL.)* We need to get out of here more often.

CARL: I agree. Too much time staring at these monitors. That'll make you crazy.

AVERY: So, anyway, my grandmother is on her deathbed, and all she wants is one thing.

CARL: *(Shrugs.)* Greens beans?

AVERY: How did you know?

CARL: Lucky guess?

AVERY: I mean, you were close. My grandmother wants green bean casserole.

JOHN: Anything for a dying grandmother, right?

AVERY: So what do I do? I rush to the store to get the ingredients for her favorite dish before she, well, before... *(Starts to cry.)* She's gone!

JOHN: *(Hands her a tissue. To CARL.)* I hate it when they cry, even when it's on camera. It always gets to me.

AVERY: *(Takes the tissue.)* Thank you.

CARL: I agree. That's why I like watching the monitors and not dealing with real people.

JOHN: But we have a real one right here.

AVERY: Sorry. *(Wipes her eyes.)* So, anyway, Grandma is in the hospital on her deathbed, and to make matters worse, Mama's at the vet with Sadie.

CARL: Sadie?

AVERY: Our dog. Sadie ate a squirrel, and it made her violently sick. Daddy's in Japan for business, my brother is away at college, so I'm the only one left to see about Grandma's dying wish.

JOHN: Green bean casserole?

AVERY: Exactly.

CARL: And Grandpa?

AVERY: He's gone. Don't even get me started on that.

JOHN: My condolences. *(To CARL.)* Should we call security?

CARL: We are security, you dummy!

AVERY: Call security for what? Looking for the ladies' room?

JOHN: No restroom in here.

AVERY: I see that now, and I'm sorry. I'm just... you know... catching my breath.

JOHN: Shopping for Grandma is hard work?

AVERY: You have no idea!

JOHN: Oh, I bet we do! I bet we do!

CARL: Nice purse.

AVERY: This? Thanks. It's Grandma's. I borrowed it.

CARL: Nice.

JOHN: Did you need to borrow something else?

AVERY: Excuse me?

CARL: I think John is asking if you borrowed it, or... you know...

AVERY: What? Stole it?

JOHN: Did you?

AVERY: No! Why would I steal my grandmother's purse?

CARL: I'm not saying you did, I'm just asking... What am I asking, John?

JOHN: He's asking, "What do you have in your purse?"

AVERY: That is none of your business!

JOHN: Do you mind if I take a look?

AVERY: Yes, I mind! A woman's purse is private!

JOHN: Please?

AVERY: Oh, my gosh! Please! Go ahead! If it thrills you, just go ahead and look in my purse!

JOHN: *(Opens her purse.)* Ah-ha!

AVERY: What?

JOHN: *(Lifts a can of green beans from her purse.)* Green beans! You shouldn't have done that, missy.

AVERY: What?

JOHN: We have you on camera. You stole this can of green beans.

AVERY: *(Suddenly nervous.)* This is what you do in here? Watch people on camera?

JOHN: Yep. And we saw your hot little fingers drop these green beans into your purse.

AVERY: By accident!

CARL: Always the same story. It fell in my purse, pocket, baby carrier, under my clothes, all by itself! Sure, sure.

AVERY: It was an accident! I was going to pay for this!

CARL: Sure, sure.

AVERY: Okay, so I realized I had no money, and Grandma was dying, and all she asked for was green bean casserole! So, yes! Yes, yes, yes, yes, yes! I did it! *(Holds out her arms.)* So, go ahead! Take me to jail for stealing food for my dying grandmother.

JOHN: *(To CARL.)* Should we?

CARL: Maybe.

JOHN: *(To AVERY.)* I have a question for you.

AVERY: I refuse to answer any questions without my attorney!

JOHN: Question. What about the cream of mushroom soup and the onions?

CARL: Hey, have you ever tried adding fresh chopped mushrooms? Makes it good!

AVERY: What?

JOHN: You can't really make green bean casserole without the other stuff, can you?

AVERY: To be honest, I hadn't finished shopping yet.

CARL: You mean, you hadn't finished stealing yet!

AVERY: *(Holds out her arms.)* Go ahead! Arrest me already!

JOHN: Should we?

CARL: Probably.

AVERY: You know, it's sad to think that I will go to jail for trying to prepare my grandmother's last meal.

JOHN: Question. What hospital?

AVERY: Trinity Medical Center.

JOHN: Her name?

AVERY: Grandma!

JOHN: Her real name?

AVERY: Grandma!

JOHN: *(Takes a deep breath.)* The name she was given at birth?

AVERY: Edna Rose Evans.

JOHN: *(Picks up the phone.)* Trinity Medical Center, please. *(To OTHERS.)* We'll just see... *(Into the phone.)* Yes, is there an Edna Rose Evans there? Uh-huh. Uh-huh. Okay. *(Hangs up.)* She's in room 520.

AVERY: Told you! And she's gravely ill.

JOHN: *(Stands and grabs a walkie-talkie.)* Let's go.

AVERY: Oh, please! Please don't lock me up!

JOHN: I'm not.

AVERY: Then where are we going?

JOHN: Shopping. I'm going to buy you some cream of mushroom soup and French-fried onions.

AVERY: You are?

CARL: Don't forget the fresh mushrooms. Then you chop them up into little pieces and stir them in. Yum!

AVERY: Fresh mushrooms. That sounds good.

JOHN: Okay, we'll get the fresh mushrooms too, then send you on your way. But next time, bring cash or a credit card.

AVERY: Yes, sir! *(THEY EXIT.)*

CARL: *(Moves chair back and returns to watching the monitor. Picks up a walkie-talkie.)* You're a pushover, John. And a good one at that. *(Short pause. Into the walkie-talkie.)* Got one! Shoplifter on aisle three. Heartburn medicine in the right pocket. Yep. He's going to need that heartburn medicine by the time we're finished with him. *(LIGHTS FADE to BLACK.)*

JOB FAIR

CAST OF CHARACTERS

ZENDA (E)..strict interviewer
KAITLIN (F).......................................self-involved job seeker
BOB (M)..nervous job seeker
JED (M) ....lazy job seeker
MEG (F)..ambitious job seeker
DAVEY (M)..under-aged job seeker

SETTING
A job fair.

PROPERTIES
Desk, two chairs, sign that reads "Job Fair Interviews." Cell phone, sheet of paper, baseball cap, bubble gum.

LIGHTS UP on ZENDA, sitting at a desk with an empty chair in front of her. A sign on the desk reads "Job Fair Interviews."

ZENDA: *(Calls OFF.)* Next. *(Waits. Calls a bit louder.)* Next. *(Waits, then stands and screams.)* Next!

KAITLIN: *(Rushes IN with a phone.)* Oh, sorry! I was on the phone fighting with my boyfriend. Ugh! He makes me so mad! Why, might you ask?

ZENDA: I didn't ask. But I do ask questions like, why should we hire you? What are your strengths? What are your weaknesses? Is being late one of your weaknesses?

KAITLIN: We'll get to that in a sec. *(Sits.)* So, anyway, Jordan was, like, so mean to me in my dream last night. And today, he can't understand why I'm so mad at him. Sure, I know it was just a dream, but it seemed real to me, you know? And I can't just get over my feelings like that. In my dream, he was screaming at me and telling me all these horrible things, and today, well... I just hate him! You know? So, he needs to apologize. Even if it was just a dream and he didn't do anything wrong.

ZENDA: *(Calls OFF.)* Next!

KAITLIN: Next? But I'm next.

ZENDA: We're done here.

KAITLIN: Done? But I haven't even had my interview yet.

ZENDA: Look, I'm here to hire people with a strong work ethic who are dependable, self-motivated, and have a positive attitude.

KAITLIN: That's me! I'm the person you're looking for!

ZENDA: You're delaying your own interview because you had a fight with your boyfriend. There's a long line over there—well, sort of—of people waiting to be interviewed for this job, and you held everyone up. Do you think your boss will overlook tardiness because you had a spat with your boyfriend?

KAITLIN: Well, I guess not. Good point. It'll never happen again, I promise.

ZENDA: Tardiness is never acceptable, at least not without a legitimate excuse. A valid excuse would be that you had jury duty, and we would need proof of that. Or that you had been kidnapped. We would need proof of that too.

KAITLIN: Kidnapped? How can I have proof of that?

ZENDA: If it's not all over the news, then you're fired.

KAITLIN: Oh. Are there any other excuses?

ZENDA: Well, if you're on your deathbed…

KAITLIN: But what if I have the flu?

ZENDA: Did you not get your flu shot? It's required. Like I said, you could be on your deathbed, but we would need proof of that, as well.

KAITLIN: What kind of company are you?

ZENDA: We specialize in farming.

KAITLIN: Oh. Well, I can type really fast, and I'm a good speller. With spellcheck, that is.

ZENDA: How do you feel about getting your hands dirty?

KAITLIN: *(Looks at her hands.)* Well, I…

ZENDA: Are you afraid of a little dirt under your fingernails?

KAITLIN: *(Holds up her hands and stares at them.)* You know, I once thought about becoming a hand model. It's legitimate. You can model rings, watches, lotion that makes your skin beautiful, different colors of nail polish. I always thought I could make a fortune doing that.

ZENDA: *(Irritated.)* Then why don't you?

KAITLIN: I might. Someday.

ZENDA: So, you don't mind, or you do?

KAITLIN: Mind what?

ZENDA: Getting dirt under your nails!

KAITLIN: You know, that's really not my thing. I make my boyfriend take care of all that kind of stuff, at least when I'm speaking to him, which I'm not right now. Oh, did I tell you what he said to me in my dream last night?

ZENDA: I couldn't care less.

KAITLIN: What?

ZENDA: Thank you for stopping by.

KAITLIN: That's it?

ZENDA: Yes. This interview is over.

KAITLIN: Don't you have another position open that's less, you know, dirty?

ZENDA: I'm afraid not. Again, thank you for stopping by. Next!

KAITLIN: *(Stands.)* Before I leave, could you at least tell me what kind of job you are interviewing for?

ZENDA: A worm digger.

KAITLIN: A worm digger? What is that?

ZENDA: I believe it's self-explanatory. You gather worms to be used as fish bait. Someone has to do it. *(Calls OFF.)* Next!

KAITLIN: Wow. Never. *(Holds up her hands.)* I should consider that hand-modeling job after all. *(Starts to leave as BOB ENTERS. To BOB.)* I hope you like getting dirt under your nails! *(EXITS.)*

BOB: What?

ZENDA: *(To BOB.)* Please, have a seat.

BOB: Thank you. *(Sits.)* I have to tell you that I get a little nervous at these things. Butterflies, I guess. It's as if... *(Looks around, then grabs the sign off the desk and fans himself with it.)* It's as if I can't breathe. Whew! Does it feel hot in here?

ZENDA: No, it doesn't.

BOB: *(Fans faster.)* Must be me. I know it's silly, but when I feel like I'm being put on the spot, I panic. Which doesn't mean I can't do the job you have available. It's just interviews. Or if I have to stand in front of people and talk. Do I have to stand in front of people and talk with this job?

ZENDA: No.

BOB: Okay, good. I'm just going to relax and take some deep breaths. *(Fans himself and takes a few deep breaths.)* It's not like I'm in trouble here. I haven't done anything wrong.

ZENDA: Something wrong?

BOB: *(Small laugh.)* It's not like you're the IRS, or the police, or my mom, or… *(Points heavenward.)* But last week…

ZENDA: You don't have to tell me.

BOB: Maybe I should get it out. Clear the soul.

ZENDA: Sir, this is a job interview.

BOB: I'll tell you, but you have to promise not to tell anyone.

ZENDA: This really isn't the time or place.

BOB: Fine! I ate all the marshmallows from the box of Lucky Charms, then lied to my kids about it. Oh, what is wrong with me?

ZENDA: I have no idea.

BOB: "Daddy, where's the marshmallows?" "I don't know, kids. I guess we got a bad box." *(Leans in.)* But it was me! I ate all the marshmallows! *(Sighs.)* Wow, that felt good. I needed to get that off my chest. *(Deep breath.)* Okay. I'm still feeling nervous, but I'm ready to begin this interview now. *(Fans himself.)*

ZENDA: Okay… Your first question is—

BOB: Yes!

ZENDA: You don't even know the question yet.

BOB: Yes! Whatever needs to be done, I'll do it! I need a job, so, yes!

ZENDA: Perfect. *(Hands him a sheet of paper.)* If you could fill out this form for HR, then you can start tomorrow night. Wear something comfortable. You'll only need a flashlight and a bucket, which will both be provided for you.

BOB: A flashlight and a bucket?

ZENDA: Yes. For gathering worms.

BOB: A worm digger?

ZENDA: Yes. We pay by the—

BOB: Oh, no! *(Stands.)* No, no, no, no, no! I don't like creepy crawly things. And slimy worms? Forget it!

ZENDA: But you just said yes.

BOB: No! In fact, never! *(Runs OFF.)*

ZENDA: *(Takes a deep breath and calls OFF.)* Next!

JED: *(ENTERS.)* Hey! What's up?

ZENDA: What's up? Well, I'm doing job interviews. How about you?

JED: Just checking them out. This job fair thing has me thinking that maybe I should get a job. *(Laughs.)* Start paying my own way. So, I thought I'd stop by and see if something interests me. *(Sits.)*

ZENDA: *(Hesitant.)* What are your interests?

JED: *(Kicks back in the chair.)* Well, let's see. I like to go with the flow, see where life takes me. And here I am. It took me here. Cool, huh?

ZENDA: Do you have any work experience?

JED: Kinda.

ZENDA: Kinda?

JED: I sold these candy bars in high school so that I could go on a band trip to Hawaii. Man, I sold a ton of those candy bars!

ZENDA: You're telling me that the only job you've ever had was a fundraiser for a school trip?

JED: Yep. I got a flower lei around my neck. Oh, and get this! I learned how to do the hula dance! *(Stands and hulas.)*

ZENDA: That's enough. Really, that's enough.

JED: Isn't this cool? I'm pretty good, aren't I?

ZENDA: Please stop.

JED: *(Stops, shrugs.)* Sorry, I got carried away. *(Sits.)*

ZENDA: It's a good thing that this job doesn't require previous experience.

JED: Cool.

ZENDA: Do you mind getting dirt under your nails?

JED: I don't know.

ZENDA: Because this job requires a little digging around in the dirt.

JED: What? Planting stuff? I don't exactly got a green thumb.

ZENDA: You don't exactly got good English, either.

JED: Well, like I said, I just go with the flow.

ZENDA: Fortunately for you, this job doesn't require proper English.

JED: What does it require, if I might so kindly inquire? See, I can speak properly if I want to.

ZENDA: You'd be digging for worms. We have a worm farm.

JED: No way!

ZENDA: Yes, it's true.

JED: Dig around for worms? Like with my hands? Like manual labor?

ZENDA: Yes. *(Sighs.)* That's what the job opening is for.

JED: No way! I'd rather flip burgers! But, really, I don't want to do that either. I'd rather make money playing video games. Yeah, that's my kind of job.

ZENDA: *(Calls OFF.)* Next!

JED: That is, if I wanted a job. You really pay people to dig for worms?

ZENDA: Since you're not interested, you may leave.

JED: Guess I never really thought about how those worms got in those little white Styrofoam containers. Wow. You pull the little slimy suckers out of the earth as they scream for mercy? Let me go! Let me go! Don't take me from my home!

ZENDA: As I said, you may leave.

JED: *(Overacts.)* Please don't stick a hook in my mouth and feed me to the fish! Please!

ZENDA: Would you please stop? *(Calls OFF.)* Next!

JED: *(Throws his arms in the air.)* Someone save me! I don't want to be used as bait!

ZENDA: Security!

JED: Okay, okay, I'm leaving. *(Stands.)* But I might just start a little petition. Save the worms! Maybe if I get a thousand signatures… *(EXITS.)*

MEG: *(ENTERS.)* Hi! Thanks for seeing me! I'm happy to have the opportunity for this interview. It means so much to me. I'm so excited about this potential move in my career! I'm ready and willing for a change, and I think this job is just what I've been looking for. Thank you, thank you so much.

ZENDA: Goodness. You're a bit excited about this job, aren't you?

MEG: Oh, yes. I love new opportunities!

ZENDA: Perfect, because I have a new opportunity for you.

MEG: Perfect!

ZENDA: Perfect. We are hiring worm diggers, and I think you're perfect for the job.

MEG: Oh, thank you, thank you so much! I'll take it. Wait... a what? Did you say a worm digger?

ZENDA: Yes. You go out at night with a flashlight and a bucket, both of which will be provided for you, and you dig around in the dirt for worms. *(MEG'S smile starts to drop.)* As an added perk, you may use headphones to listen to whatever music or podcast you'd like while you work. Ready to get started? *(Holds up a piece of paper.)* We just need you to fill this out for HR.

MEG: What's the starting salary?

ZENDA: Actually, we pay by the worm.

MEG: I need to make a big career move right now if I want to stay on my five-year plan to make six figures. This might not be the perfect opportunity for me after all, but thank you, anyway. *(Runs OFF.)*

ZENDA: *(Calls OFF, hopeless.)* Next. If there is a next...

DAVEY: *(ENTERS, chomping gum. He wears a baseball cap backwards and his shoelaces are untied.)* Hello.

ZENDA: Hello. Are you here to inquire about the job?

DAVEY: Sure.

ZENDA: Great. Have a seat. *(DAVEY sits down and blows a bubble.)* First question. Are you afraid of insects and bugs?

DAVEY: No way. I love them!

ZENDA: But do you love them so much that you want to save them?

DAVEY: Save them?

ZENDA: Because you consider them to be little pets.

DAVEY: I mean, I've kept them as pets before, but that was a couple of years ago.

ZENDA: So you don't mind if they die?

DAVEY: No way! I'd step on them in a heartbeat. Oooh, look at the guts! Cool, huh?

ZENDA: Great. Are you afraid of getting dirt under your fingernails?

DAVEY: No way. *(Looks at his hands.)* I have dirt under my nails right now. See?

ZENDA: Yes, you do. Well, so far, so good. Let me cut to the chase. I have a job opening for a worm digger.

DAVEY: Oh, cool. That's super cool! I could do that.

ZENDA: You will?

DAVEY: Yeah! Sure, I will! What does it pay?

ZENDA: You get paid per worm. Our rates are on the higher end than most worm farms.

DAVEY: Awesome! *(Stands and calls OFF.)* Mom! Mom! Hey, Mom! I got a job digging for worms!

ZENDA: Uh… wait a minute. How old are you?

DAVEY: What does that matter? I am kind of tall for my age, but that's a plus, right?

ZENDA: It matters. This job would be forty hours per week.

DAVEY: I do have school, and I need time to hang out with my friends, but I can work on Saturdays.

ZENDA: You're a minor, aren't you?

DAVEY: Hey, I'm practically a teenager! Just a couple of months.

ZENDA: *(Calls OFF.)* Next!

DAVEY: Cool! I get to play with worms and get paid for it!

ZENDA: *(Calls OFF.)* Next!

DAVEY: *(Pretends to pull a worm from the dirt.)* Hello, my little slimy friend! *(LIGHTS FADE to BLACK.)*

———○———

DELAYED

CAST OF CHARACTERS

SYLVIA (F) .... stranded passenger
WHITNEY (F) .... another
CHARLES (M) .... another

SETTING
An airport gate waiting area.

PROPERTIES
Three chairs. Two cell phones, carry-on bags, purse with tissues.

SOUND EFFECTS
Two different ringtones.

LIGHTS UP on SYLVIA, WHITNEY, and CHARLES, sitting next to each other at an airport waiting for their flight, which keeps getting delayed. SYLVIA and WHITNEY are looking at their phones, and CHARLES sits between them, sleeping with his head down.

SYLVIA: *(Looks up.)* Did you get that text? Our flight is delayed again.

WHITNEY: I just saw that. Great.

SYLVIA: I hate traveling. The lines. The waiting. The more waiting. *(CHARLES begins snoring loudly.)* Not to mention the people! *(They both stare at him. Another loud snore.)*

WHITNEY: Wow. That's really loud. Should I nudge him?

SYLVIA: Yes! Please, do! *(WHITNEY nudges CHARLES with her elbow. He jumps, looks around, then quickly goes back to sleep. The women shrug.)* Exciting trip planned?

WHITNEY: No, not really. A funeral.

SYLVIA: Oh! Oh, I'm so sorry. My condolences.

WHITNEY: It's no big deal.

SYLVIA: Distant relative? Great, great uncle, or something like that?

WHITNEY: My mother's cat.

SYLVIA: A cat funeral?

WHITNEY: Unfortunately. *(CHARLES drops his head onto WHITNEY'S shoulder. She freezes.)* Wow. This is awkward.

SYLVIA: I'd laugh, but... I won't.

WHITNEY: Thanks. What should I do?

SYLVIA: Smack him? That's what I'd do. *(CHARLES snuggles in and snores louder.)*

WHITNEY: Oh, my gosh! I can't take this!

SYLVIA: I know! On the count of three, lean forward as if you're getting something out of your bag.

WHITNEY: Good idea.

SYLVIA: One... two... three. *(WHITNEY leans forward.)*

CHARLES: *(Falls over and wakes up from a dream.)* Mama? Mama? Where are you? *(Looks around, confused, then leans back in his chair and goes back to sleep. The girls give each other a look and mouth, "Mama"?)*

WHITNEY: So, anyway, Mom's cat is... I mean, was... fourteen years old. Lucy. Lucy loved no one but my mom. And let me tell you, Lucy was a little terror. *(Hisses.)* She hissed at me, hissed at my dad, hissed at anyone that came over. *(Leans toward SYLVIA.)* Just between you and me, I hated that cat.

SYLVIA: Well, that's nice of you to attend the funeral considering that you hated her. *(SOUND EFFECT: WHITENEY'S PHONE RINGS.)*

WHITNEY: *(Answers her phone.)* Hi, Mom. Listen, my flight was delayed again... I'm sorry! Look, Lucy won't know I'm late to her funeral. *(Listens.)* I know, Mom! I know I'm a pallbearer. But seriously, Mom, who plans an elaborate funeral for a dumb... *(Quickly catches herself.)* ...I mean, precious cat? *(Covers the phone. To SYLVIA.)* I hate that cat! *(Into the phone.)* I'm sorry, Mom. Tell them to sing a few extra songs, and I'll get there as fast as I can. *(Hangs up.)* I hate that cat.

SYLVIA: *(Sweetly.)* But you love your mom.

CHARLES: *(Stretches and yawns, waking up.)* I'm a dog person myself. *(SYLVIA and WHITNEY exchange looks.)* My dog, well, he hates cats!

SYLVIA: I've heard dogs and cats can learn to get along.

CHARLES: Nope. Not my dog. He'd never get along with a cat.

WHITNEY: Well, Lucy would never get along with your dog. She'd scratch his eyes out if he even dared come close.

SYLVIA: *(Snickers.)* Bet that would send him yelping back home. *(To WHITNEY.)* I'm sorry. I didn't even ask your name. I'm Sylvia. *(Offers her hand.)*

WHITNEY: *(Takes her hand.)* I'm Whitney.

SYLVIA: Nice to meet you, Whitney.

CHARLES: I'm Charles.

WHITNEY/SYLVIA: Nice to meet you, Charles.

WHITNEY: So, Sylvia, do you have any pets? I don't, thanks to Lucy for giving me pet issues. *(CHARLES closes his eyes as if to go back to sleep.)*

SYLVIA: I have a fish. A sweet little goldfish.

WHITNEY: Aw... that sounds like my kind of pet. A little pinch of food, and you're done. No walking. No scooping a litter box. No trips to the vet.

CHARLES: *(Eyes closed.)* Good for bait, if you ask me. Stick 'em on a hook! Gone fishin'!

SYLVIA: Excuse me?!

CHARLES: *(Opens his eyes.)* Oh, sorry. I was drifting. You know, half asleep, half awake. I don't know what I was saying. Sorry. I'll just go back to sleep. *(Leans back and closes his eyes.)*

WHITNEY: So, anyway, I think a fish would be a perfect pet.

SYLVIA: Yes. And I know he's just a little fish, but he seems to know me. Every morning when I go to feed him, his little tail dances in the water.

WHITNEY: Aw...

SYLVIA: An easy little pet, for sure. I've had him for about a year. Little precious...

CHARLES: *(Opens his eyes.)* Hey! My dog's name is Precious!

SYLVIA: *(Smiles.)* Really?

CHARLES: Yeah! But he's mean and vicious, unlike your Precious. *(Laughs.)* He'd gobble up your Precious in one quick—

WHITNEY: *(Snaps at him.)* Stop that!

CHARLES: Oh! Sorry! Really. I'm sorry. *(SOUND EFFECT: WHITNEY'S PHONE RINGS.)*

WHITNEY: *(Answers her phone.)* No, Mom. I'm still sitting at the airport... *(Listens.)* I know, Mom, but I can't control when the plane leaves... *(Listens.)* No, I can't talk to the pilot and tell him this is an emergency... *(Listens.)* Mom, I know! *(Listens.)* Mom, I can't help it! *(Listens.)* Mom, she's dead! I'm sorry... *(Listens.)* Mom, I'm sorry. I'm sorry your cat went over the Rainbow Bridge. *(Listens.)* Okay. I'll let you know right before I take off.

CHARLES: Rainbow Bridge? *(Laughs. To SYLVIA.)* Do you think your goldfish can swim over that Rainbow Bridge? My dog, well, he doesn't do rainbows. *(Loud.)* Because he's mean and tough and will eat anything in his sight! Especially shoes.

SYLVIA: *(Sarcastic.)* Sounds precious.

CHARLES: He is. *(SOUND EFFECT: SYLVIA'S PHONE RINGS.)*

SYLVIA: *(Answers her phone.)* Hello? *(Listens.)* What? What do you mean he's floating upside down? Oh, no!

WHITNEY: What's wrong?

SYLVIA: *(Into the phone. In tears.)* Okay... *(Listens.)* Okay, bye. *(Puts her phone down.)* My friend went over to feed my fish and... *(Shakes her head.)*

CHARLES: Sounds like your fishie bit the dust. Dang. Sorry. Seriously, I was only joking about him swimming over that Rainbow Bridge. Guess he did just that. But just think, he's in a better place. Like a big beautiful ocean with other little fishies. *(Sings.)* Swimming in the water, swimming in the water, swimming in the water—

WHITNEY: Stop it! *(To SYLVIA.)* Are you okay?

SYLVIA: *(Cries.)* Precious is gone!

CHARLES: Wow. What a coincidence. Your fish is with her mom's mean cat. Hmm. I wonder if cats and fish get along after they go over the Rainbow Bridge? I mean, I always heard cats liked to eat fish. *(SYLVIA wails.)*

WHITNEY: Some people are so insensitive. Sylvia, if it makes you feel any better, you could have a little funeral for him when you get back home.

CHARLES: Yeah! One flush and... bye-bye!

SYLVIA: *(Horrified.)* I'm not flushing Precious!

WHITNEY: Of course, you're not! *(Glares at CHARLES, then back to SYLVIA.)* A little celebration of his life might be nice.

SYLVIA: I think you're right. I wonder if he died because he missed me? From a broken heart! *(Cries.)*

CHARLES: *(Laughing, but trying not to.)* Sorry. Really, I'm sorry. *(SOUND EFFECT: WHITNEY'S PHONE RINGS.)*

WHITNEY: *(Answers her phone.)* Mom? *(Listens.)* What? Everyone is waiting on me...? *(Listens.)* How many people are there? *(Listens.)* Forty? Wow... all dressed in black. *(Looks at her watch.)* It's going to be a couple more hours, Mom, at least. *(Hangs up.)*

CHARLES: Yeah, I'd be sad if my Precious went to doggie heaven.

SYLVIA: *(Wails.)* Oh, Precious!

WHITNEY: *(Reaches across and takes her hand.)* I'm sorry for your loss.

CHARLES: *(Suddenly sad.)* With you crying over your Precious, well, it makes me think of my Precious. And with all this Rainbow Bridge talk... well, I... *(Starts to tear up.)* I don't think I could ever handle that. And my Precious is getting up in his years. He's fourteen years old.

WHITNEY: That's old for a dog. Lucy was fourteen.

CHARLES: Really? She was fourteen too? *(WHITNEY nods. CHARLES wipes his eyes.)* I never thought about him passing before, but now... Do either of you have a tissue? *(WHITNEY looks in her purse and hands CHARLES and SYLVIA tissues.)*

CHARLES: Thank you.

SYLVIA: Thank you. *(Gets out a pen and paper.)* I think I will plan a funeral for next Friday. Anyone want to come?

WHITNEY: I can. I'll be back from my mom's by then. Do you want me to sing a song? I don't mind.

SYLVIA: Yes. Thank you.

CHARLES: Heck, put me down too. I can do the ceremony. "We are gathered here today to remember the life of this precious little goldfish…"

SYLVIA: You'd do that?

CHARLES: Sure, I would! Guess all this talk of dying pets has made me recognize how lucky I am to still have my Precious.

SYLVIA: Thank you. *(Hands a piece of paper to each of them.)* Here's my address. Friday at ten a.m.

CHARLES: I'll be there in a coat and tie. Black, of course.

WHITNEY: I'll wear black too. *(ALL reflect, sad.)*

CHARLES: *(Then, suddenly.)* Floating upside down in the water, huh? *(SYLVIA wails. SOUND EFFECT: WHITNEY'S PHONE RINGS.)*

WHITNEY: *(Answers her phone.)* Mom, I'm still at the airport! I'll get there as fast as I can! *(CHARLES leans back, closes his eyes, and begins to snore. LIGHTS FADE to BLACK.)*

STRANGE ADDICTIONS

CAST OF CHARACTERS

BETH (E) .... addiction counselor
EARL (M) ....collects toenails
MIKE (M) ....obsessively calls his mom
SUE (F) ....thinks she is a cat

SETTING
A meeting room.
PROPERTIES
High back chair, three small chairs, potted plant. Cell phone, small snack, plastic bag, nail clippers.

LIGHTS UP on BETH, sitting in a large office chair CENTER. MIKE, SUE, and EARL sit in smaller chairs facing her. SUE is between MIKE and EARL.

BETH: Welcome. Welcome to Strange Addictions Anonymous. SAA, if you prefer. Here, you are free to share your most private and hidden addictions. And please, please be assured that you don't need to fear being misunderstood or judged, because here, we listen and support one another. No matter the addiction. Also, a quick reminder, no laughing is allowed. You may nod your head to show your support or ask a question to further understand the problem, but absolutely no laughter or negative comments.

EARL: What about you? Are you addicted to anything?

BETH: Actually, yes. Thank you for asking. Exercise. Excessive exercise. To the point that it was once controlling my life.

EARL: Were you able to stop exercising?

BETH: Good question. What I was able to do was set limits. Thirty minutes a day. But, do I ever have stressful times and slip back into the excessive workouts to the point where

I want to do jumping jacks or jog in place for hours on end? Or worse yet, at inappropriate places? Say, a business meeting or a movie theater or a funeral?

MIKE: You did jumping jacks at a funeral?

BETH: *(Raises her hand.)* Guilty. And that's why we're here, to acknowledge that we have a problem and then support and encourage each other as we work through our own issues. So, let's begin. Who would like to go first?

MIKE: *(Halfway raises his hand.)* I guess I can go.

BETH: Wonderful. What is your name?

MIKE: Mike.

ALL: Hi, Mike.

MIKE: Hi.

BETH: So, tell us about your addiction, Mike.

MIKE: *(Quiet.)* Well, I... I call my mom.

BETH: You call her names?

MIKE: No, of course not! *(Holds up his phone.)* I call my mom.

BETH: Oh, on the phone.

MIKE: That's right.

BETH: Well, that seems quite normal.

MIKE: But I call her a lot.

BETH: A lot?

MIKE: Yes. I like to hear her voice. Constantly. It's comforting, soothing, like when I was a baby.

BETH: I see.

SUE: How many times do you call her?

MIKE: A lot.

SUE: Well, I call my mom four or five times a day, and that seems like a lot, but I don't think it's strange.

BETH: Mike, could you be more specific about how often you call her?

MIKE: I already told you. A lot. We hang up, and I call her again. And again. And again.

EARL: And she answers?

MIKE: Not always, but most of the time, yes, because if she doesn't I keep calling her. Again and again and again.

EARL: Oh, brother! What a...

BETH: Now, now! No judging or name calling. We all have issues here that we are dealing with. We're here to help, support, and offer ideas to break these chains that are our addictions.

SUE: I have an idea.

BETH: Yes, Sue?

SUE: Why don't you tell your mom to get a new phone number and not tell you what it is?

EARL: *(Laughs.)* Yeah! I love that idea!

SUE: Then all you will hear is "We're sorry. You have reached a number that has been disconnected or is no longer in service."

EARL: Great idea!

SUE: Thank you.

MIKE: But what if I need my mom?

EARL: Then drive to her house and talk to her.

MIKE: She lives three hundred fifty miles away.

SUE: Oh, then that's definitely a problem.

BETH: Mike, have you tried putting your phone away and limiting yourself to just one phone call per day?

MIKE: Tried it. It didn't work. *(Without thinking, calls his mom. Into phone.)* Hello, Mom... I did. I'm here... Well, I miss you... I know, Mom, but I can't do this without you...

EARL: Oh, brother!

BETH: Mike, can you hang up now, please?

MIKE: I'm talking to my mom! *(Talks quieter.)* I got into trouble... Okay, hold on... *(To BETH.)* Mom wants to know why I'm in trouble.

BETH: You're not in trouble, Mike. It's just that we need to continue with our meeting, so, if you don't mind, can you call her back later?

MIKE: *(Into the phone.)* Did you hear that, Mom?... Yeah. I have to hang up... Okay. I'll call you back later. Love you. *(Hangs up.)*

BETH: Mike, can you please hand me your phone? I promise I'll give it back at the end of our session. *(MIKE hands her the phone, and she sets it under her chair.)* Okay, who's next?

SUE: *(Raises her hand.)* I guess me.

BETH: Tell us your name.

SUE: I'm Sue.

ALL: Hi, Sue.

BETH: Welcome, Sue.

SUE: Thank you.

BETH: Tell us about your addiction.

SUE: Cats.

EARL: *(Points.)* Hey, it's a cat lady!

BETH: Please, let's not point and ridicule. Go on, Sue.

SUE: *(Shoots EARL a look.)* Well, I have thirteen cats. There's Juliet, Bishop, Sophie, Lilly, Tom, Simba, Max, Whiskers, Tango, Iris, Snowball, Sugar, and Blackie.

BETH: Thirteen. Goodness. You must love your little fur babies a lot.

SUE: I do, but that's not the problem.

BETH: Go on.

SUE: Well, I... *(MIKE starts using his foot to try to get the phone from under BETH'S chair.)* I don't get out much so I... I mean, I mostly stay indoors with my cats, and I... well, you see, I... I don't like to leave them, and I... I feel like we're family, you know... like we're connected... and I... well... I...

EARL: Just say it already!

BETH: *(Shoots EARL a look, then turns back to SUE.)* Yes?

SUE: Well, I... *(Suddenly begins meowing like a cat.)* Meow, meow, meow...

EARL: What the heck? *(Points.)* She thinks she's a cat! *(Claps.)* That's hilarious!

MIKE: *(Finally gets the phone.)* I'm calling my mom! She'll love this. *(Dials.)*

BETH: *(To MIKE.)* Put that down! *(To EARL.)* Remember, Earl, we don't make fun of others or criticize. We encourage and offer helpful advice.

MIKE: *(Into the phone.)* Mom...

BETH: Mike, can't you call her later?

SUE: Meow, meow, meow...

MIKE: *(Into the phone.)* No, there's not a cat in here. Well, I mean, there's a lady who thinks she's a cat... I know. It's weird.

SUE: Do you have any treats? I like treats. Those little square ones are my favorite. You can toss a few on the ground, if you don't have a bowl.

EARL: This is hilarious!

BETH: *(Snaps her fingers at EARL.)* Stop that! No negative talk!

MIKE: Hold on, Mom. *(To SUE.)* Is it true? You think you're a cat?

SUE: Meow.

MIKE: *(Into the phone.)* Yeah, she's a cat.

BETH: Mike, can you call your mother back later?

MIKE: *(To BETH.)* Hold on! *(Takes a small snack out of his pocket and tosses it on the ground.)* Here, kitty, kitty, kitty...

SUE: *(Excitedly jumps on the ground and sniffs the snack.)* Hey! These aren't the treats I like!

MIKE: Mom, do you want another cat? She seems friendly enough.

BETH: *(Holds out her hand.)* Mike, give me the phone, please. You can call her back later.

MIKE: Mom, I have to go! The counselor says I have to call you back. Whatever!

BETH: Why don't you call her back tomorrow?

MIKE: Tomorrow? I can't wait that long! *(Into the phone.)* Mom, I'll call you back in a sec... Okay. Love you too. *(Hangs up.)*

BETH: *(Still holding out her hand.)* Phone?

MIKE: No worries. I'll just put it right here. Out of sight, out of mind. *(Places the phone under his chair.)*

BETH: Sue, perhaps this is the first step for you. Getting out of your house and socializing with uh... other humans.

SUE: *(Rubs against EARL'S leg.)* Meow.

EARL: Oh, my gosh! Make her stop! She's rubbing against me like a cat! Look here, lady, I don't like cats! In fact, I'm allergic to them! *(Sneezes. SUE hisses.)* Did you see that? She hissed at me!

MIKE: *(Grabs his phone and dials, unable to control himself. Into the phone.)* Mom, it's getting weird in here... I know it's for strange addictions, but I shouldn't be here! So what if I call you a few hundred times a day? Okay, I'll pay attention... Love you too. *(Hangs up.)*

BETH: *(Holds her hand out to MIKE.)* Why don't you let me hold that for you?

MIKE: Nope. Out of sight, out of mind. *(Looks around for another hiding spot and hides it behind a plant in the corner.)* There we go. *(Sits back down.)*

BETH: *(To EARL.)* Why don't we discuss why you're here? *(SUE hisses at EARL.)*

EARL: Can you make her stop hissing at me?

BETH: Calm down, Sue. We're all here to support each other.

SUE: I'm tired! I need a nap! *(Curls up and goes to sleep on the floor.)*

EARL: Great. She's purring now. Okay, well, I'm Earl.

BETH/MIKE: Hi, Earl.

BETH: Tell us about your addiction.

MIKE: Can I call my mom for a second?

BETH: No. Go ahead, Earl.

EARL: Toenails.

MIKE: What? You paint them?

EARL: No. I collect them.

BETH: You collect toenails?

EARL: Yeah. I mean, after I cut them, of course.

MIKE: Weird. I've got to tell my mom about this. *(Sneaks over to the plant.)*

BETH: No calls right now. *(MIKE FREEZES. It's killing him not to grab the phone.)*

EARL: Well, I started doing this when I was seven years old. I thought I'd make a toenail collection. Pretty cool, huh?

MIKE: Stupid, if you ask me.

BETH: Remember, we are not here to judge.

EARL: So, I started putting them in this old tin box. That was twenty years ago. Man! You should see how many I have now! Wish I could sell them on eBay. Think they're worth anything?

MIKE: No.

BETH: Have you thought about throwing them in the trash?

EARL: That's what my wife said. You sound kind of like my wife. But I said, "Heck no! Do you know how long I've been collecting my toenails?" And you know what she said? "It's either them or me!" So, either I throw them away, or she leaves me!

SUE: *(Wakes up and stretches.)* Why are you yelling? You woke me up! I'm so tired!

EARL: Then go back to sleep!

SUE: *(Hisses at EARL.)* I don't want to now. *(Smiles, purrs, and licks her hands.)*

EARL: *(Sneezes.)* I told you I'm allergic to cats!

MIKE: *(Grabs the phone and dials.)* Mom, these people are weird with a capital W.

BETH: Please call your mother later.

MIKE: *(Into the phone.)* I don't know. Between the human cat and the toenail collector, I'm starting to freak out.

BETH: Hang up, please.

MIKE: *(Glares at BETH.)* I have to go, Mom! Love you too. *(Doesn't hang up.)*

BETH: So, Earl, what do you love the most? Your old toenails or your wife?

EARL: And that's the question of the day.

BETH: Well?

EARL: I'm telling you the truth. It's a hard decision for me. I mean, I love my toenail collection. And my friends, at least up to junior high, all thought my collection was cool!

BETH: Seriously? You don't know if you love your wife more than your clipped toenails? *(SUE swipes at EARL.)*

EARL: Did you see that? She just swiped me with her… her claws!

MIKE: *(Into the phone.)* Mom! I think I'm going to exit early! These people are weird!

BETH: Hang up!

MIKE: Gotta go! Love you too! *(Pretends to hang up.)*

BETH: Earl, let's unpack this.

EARL: Okay.

BETH: Why did you start collecting your toenails?

EARL: Because it was fun!

BETH: Fun?

EARL: Yes! Oh, and I brought some of them—the toenails I've clipped while in therapy. *(Pulls out a plastic bag from his pocket.)* Want to see?

BETH: No! No! Please, no! *(SUE hisses.)*

MIKE: I do.

BETH: I have a better idea. Let's imagine that your wife is here.

EARL: *(Sarcastic.)* Oh, great.

BETH: Put down the Baggie and picture your wife sitting next to you. Now think. Think real hard. Who can you throw your arms around? Who can you kiss? Who makes you feel wonderful on the inside?

EARL: *(Grabs the plastic bag and holds it tightly.)* I'm keeping my toenails! *(Lifts the Baggie and kisses it.)* I love you! I love you! I love you! *(SUE hisses and swipes him again. To SUE.)* Stop that! Bad kitty! Bad, bad kitty!

MIKE: *(Into the phone.)* Mom, this guy in here loves his toenails more than his wife.

BETH: Hang up the phone! Now!

MIKE: Love you! *(Hangs up. SUE yawns and curls up for another nap.)*

EARL: *(Takes off his shoes and socks, then pulls out clippers from his pocket.)* Let's just collect some more. Technically, this is group therapy, so they can still go in this bag. *(Cuts his toenails.)*

MIKE: *(Dials.)* Mom, I don't like it here. These people are strange. Mom, what are you doing? I miss you.

EARL: I love collecting toenails! *(Drops a clipping in the plastic bag.)*

BETH: *(Jumps up.)* You people! I just don't know what to say! *(Begins doing jumping jacks.)* No one is listening to me! How can I help you if you won't listen to me? Do I care? Maybe I only care about myself! About getting into shape. Yes, that's what I care about!

EARL: *(Holds up a clipped toenail.)* Look at this one! *(SUE continues to nap and purrs loudly.)*

MIKE: *(Into the phone.)* Mom, I know it's a long drive, but can you come pick me up? I don't think this is working.

BETH: That's it, I'm out of here! *(Jogs OFF.)*

EARL: Man, that is one strange lady! *(LIGHTS FADE to BLACK.)*

FREE ADVICE

CAST OF CHARACTERS

CHRIS (M)..college student
JOE (M)..troubled passer-by
OLIVIA (F) ....another
BERT (E) ....another
JEWEL (F) ....wise passer-by

SETTING
A street corner.

PROPERTIES
Sign that reads "Free Advice" on one side and "Free Kisses" on the other.

LIGHTS UP on CHRIS, holding a sign that reads "Free Advice."

JOE: *(ENTERS and walks past CHRIS, then stops and turns back around.)* Free advice?

CHRIS: Yes.

JOE: Are you a licensed therapist?

CHRIS: You could say that.

JOE: And it's free?

CHRIS: Completely.

JOE: Okay. Then I need some advice.

CHRIS: All right. Lay it on me.

JOE: Tell me, should I marry Sophie?

CHRIS: Do you love her?

JOE: Yes, of course I love her.

CHRIS: Can you tolerate her bad habits?

JOE: What bad habits?

CHRIS: You haven't been together long, have you?

JOE: Two months.

CHRIS: Are you ready for my advice?

JOE: You're going to say no, aren't you?

CHRIS: You should date for at least a year.

JOE: So, it's a no?

CHRIS: I try to stay away from a hard yes or no. I want to steer you in the right direction, help you to analyze the situation for yourself.

JOE: So, it's a no? No, I shouldn't marry Sophie?

CHRIS: Let me ask you this. Why do you want to marry Sophie?

JOE: Why? Because I love her! Desperately!

CHRIS: Why?

JOE: Why?

CHRIS: Yes. Why?

JOE: Because! Because she's... she's beautiful!

CHRIS: You're going to marry someone for their looks?

JOE: And she's sweet. Well, most of the time. Except for when she's bossy. But she's only bossy when she knows what's best for me. Except for yesterday...

CHRIS: What happened yesterday?

JOE: She picked out the clothes I should wear, which was a little weird.

CHRIS: What about today? Did she pick out the clothes you're wearing today?

JOE: Yes. She also said I need to buy new ones. Clothes that she likes. Because she knows what looks best on me.

CHRIS: And you don't?

JOE: I thought I did.

CHRIS: So, why else do you want to marry Sophie?

JOE: Well, she's a very clean person. You know, a clean freak. Everything has to be in its place. You know, organized. Lined up. Perfectly. And preferably labeled. *(Mimics her, waging a finger at CHRIS.)* And don't you dare leave a drawer open. Not even a tad bit, because that will drive me insane. Do you hear me? *(Yells.)* Shut the damn drawer! *(Calms down.)* Sorry.

CHRIS: Sophie likes things in their proper place?

JOE: Oh, yes! Yes, yes, yes! If you use dishes, you wash them and put them away. Immediately. If you take off your shoes, you put them away. Immediately. And if you drop an itty, bitty, tiny, little crumb on the floor, you pick it up and put it in the trash.

CHRIS: Immediately?

JOE: *(Mimics.)* Immediately!

CHRIS: Do you tend to be a perfectionist yourself?

JOE: No! Are you kidding? I'm a slob! Well, I was a slob. Until now. Sophie has changed me.

CHRIS: And does that make you happy?

JOE: I don't know. I guess.

CHRIS: Question. Whose idea was it to get married?

JOE: Hers.

CHRIS: And you're asking me if you should marry her?

JOE: *(Leans in.)* Tell me I shouldn't, okay?

CHRIS: You shouldn't.

JOE: *(Hugs him.)* Oh, thank you! Thank you! I knew it! *(Continues on his way.)* I knew it was a bad idea to marry Sophie. I can pick out my own clothes, thank you very much! And tonight, I'm going to eat pizza and let the crumbs fall wherever they may! And I'm not going to pick them up! Yes! *(EXITS as he sings.)* Freedom!

OLIVIA: *(ENTERS and sees the sign.)* I'll take some free advice.

CHRIS: How may I help you?

OLIVIA: *(Flips her hair.)* Cut it or keep it long?

CHRIS: Your hair?

OLIVIA: Yes. Cut it or keep it long?

CHRIS: What do you like?

OLIVIA: What do you like?

CHRIS: It's not my hair.

OLIVIA: But don't you have an opinion? *(Taps on his sign.)* Advice?

CHRIS: Let me ask you a question.

OLIVIA: Okay.

CHRIS: Why do you want to cut your hair?

OLIVIA: I want to try something different.

CHRIS: Expand on that, please.

OLIVIA: Well... *(Flips her hair.)* I want to get noticed.

CHRIS: You're not noticed now?

OLIVIA: Did you notice me?

CHRIS: I did.

OLIVIA: *(Leans in.)* In a good way or a bad way?

CHRIS: I'm neutral.

OLIVIA: Ah-ha! Take me or leave me, huh? Look right past me, huh? Because see, I want to get noticed! Like, "Look at her!"

CHRIS: And you believe that a new haircut will do just that?

OLIVIA: Maybe.

CHRIS: Do you like short hair?

OLIVIA: Sure. It's cute and sassy and fun.

CHRIS: And long hair?

OLIVIA: I like that too. It makes you want to reach out and touch it. Or braid it. Or just admire it.

CHRIS: So, you're undecided?

OLIVIA: Yes, that's why I'm talking to you. *(Taps on the sign.)* For free advice. So, what should I do? Tell me. Keep it long or chop it off?

CHRIS: Question.

OLIVIA: Again?

CHRIS: Work with me here. Look down and imagine your hair is on the ground. You've cut it all off. It's there. On the ground. How do you feel? Excited? Scared? Or are you crying?

OLIVIA: My hair is there? On the ground?

CHRIS: Yes. You cut it off. Do you like your new sassy bob or are you panicked, wondering if you can glue it back on until it grows back?

OLIVIA: Can I glue it back on?

CHRIS: No, though they do make extensions. But I've heard they're expensive and not good for your hair.

OLIVIA: *(Jumps back and shakes her head.)* No! No! I'm not going to do it!

CHRIS: It's nice to have options.

OLIVIA: What was I thinking? Thanks. *(Starts away.)* I think. *(EXITS.)*

BERT: *(ENTERS, sees the sign, and stops.)* Free?

CHRIS: Free.

BERT: Cool. I like free. So, I have a question for you.

CHRIS: Okay.

BERT: Should I get my own place or stay rent-free at my mom and dad's?

CHRIS: Question.

BERT: I know what you're going to ask me. "How old are you?"

CHRIS: How old are you?

BERT: That shouldn't matter. Besides, my parents offered. Well, kind of. I mean, Mom says I'll always be her baby. I like that. But Dad says I need to grow up. You know, get a job, quit playing video games all day, get my own place...

CHRIS: What do you want?

BERT: Well, free rent is nice. Plus, Mom does my laundry, cleans my room, cooks for me... you know, all that stuff.

CHRIS: And how do you feel about yourself?

BERT: Honestly? I feel like a bit of a moocher.

CHRIS: Well, then...?

BERT: *(Paces.)* But get my own place? A job? Become a responsible adult? I don't know. That's kind of scary.

CHRIS: Question. Where do you see yourself in five years?

BERT: Good question. Hmm... I'm not sure.

CHRIS: Take a wild guess.

BERT: Probably where I'm at now. I'm not saying that's good or anything, but gosh, Mom makes the best meatloaf ever. And I do kind of like her doing my laundry. Plus, Dad gives me money whenever I need it.

CHRIS: College?

BERT: Nah. I already tried that. Didn't like it and dropped out. It was hard! So, you know what? I guess I don't need any advice. I think I'll stay right where I'm at. *(Starts to leave.)* Living the good life... oh, yeah. *(EXITS. CHRIS stands alone for a moment and then sees JEWEL in the distance. He flips the sign around, and it now reads "Free Kisses.")*

JEWEL: *(ENTERS, notices the sign, and stops.)* Really? I've heard of free hugs, but free kisses? Why would you do that? *(CHRIS shrugs.)* What if an old lady comes by? Ha! And what if she takes you up on that and slips you the tongue? Ha! That'd serve you right!

CHRIS: I saw you coming my way.

JEWEL: And if I'd been an old lady? *(CHRIS flips the sign back around.)* Oh! Well, I like that. Is that for real? Free advice?

CHRIS: Yes. Or… *(Starts to flip the sign.)*

JEWEL: Oh, no, thank you. I'll take the free advice though. But first, I have a question for you.

CHRIS: Go ahead. I'm all ears.

JEWEL: Tell me, what kind of person stands on a street corner holding a sign offering free advice? Or kisses?

CHRIS: *(Smiles.)* Me.

JEWEL: Question.

CHRIS: Uh-oh. I think you're onto me.

JEWEL: Do you feel good about this activity?

CHRIS: Let me think…

JEWEL: Here's another question. Isn't the truth of the matter that you are acting out what you actually need yourself?

CHRIS: Kisses?

JEWEL: No! Advice! *(Crosses her arms.)* Lay it on me.

CHRIS: A kiss?

JEWEL: No, you moron! Your dilemma!

CHRIS: But I don't have a dilemma.

JEWEL: Then why are you doing this?

CHRIS: It's for my thesis.

JEWEL: Your thesis? A college paper?

CHRIS: Yes. "The Investigation of Counseling Accepted If Offered for Free." My theory is that most people are struggling, and they desire to seek professional help, but the finances just aren't available.

JEWEL: Oh. Well, that's interesting. A thoughtful college guy, huh?

CHRIS: So, do you need advice? It's free. *(Smiles.)* Or, if you prefer… *(Flips the sign.)*

JEWEL: But what's the point of this? Free kisses? Another paper you're writing?

CHRIS: *(Shrugs.)* No. Just a shimmer of hope in a broken world.

JEWEL: Well, maybe I do need advice.

CHRIS: *(Flips the sign.)* Great!

JEWEL: Tell me. How can I tell a certain someone... What's your name?

CHRIS: Chris.

JEWEL: Chris, how can I tell a certain someone... no names mentioned...

CHRIS: Of course not.

JEWEL: That kisses shouldn't be free except for children or relatives?

CHRIS: I say, you should be completely honest. Honesty is always the best policy.

JEWEL: Okay. Because you see, kisses are worth something.

CHRIS: Explain.

JEWEL: They're worth all the stars in the sky. The butterflies in your stomach. They should be anticipated. Dreamt about. Longed for. Timed. Protected. Committed.

CHRIS: I never thought about it like that. But I think you're right.

JEWEL: So, then, that's my advice to you. Because honesty is always the best policy.

CHRIS: Thank you. Advice taken.

JEWEL: Good. Well, have a good day giving out free advice. Or kisses... *(Starts to go.)*

CHRIS: Wait! Wait!

JEWEL: *(Stops.)* Yes?

CHRIS: I have some advice for you.

JEWEL: I'm listening.

CHRIS: You should agree to have dinner with me tonight.

JEWEL: Oh, really? But I didn't hear you ask me to have dinner tonight.

CHRIS: Will you have dinner with me tonight?

JEWEL: *(Short pause.)* Yes.

CHRIS: Wow. That was easy. Great! Then maybe, just maybe... *(Flips the sign and smiles.)* Can I get your number?

JEWEL: *(Smiles.)* Sure. *(LIGHTS FADE to BLACK.)*

HOMECOMING QUEEN

CAST OF CHARACTERS

DEREK (M).. helpful little brother
EMMA (F)..............Derek's sister; homecoming queen hopeful
BRANDON (M) ....Emma's date for homecoming
MOM (F)...Derek and Emma's mom
DAD (M)...Derek and Emma's dad

SETTING
Emma's bedroom.

PROPERTIES
Bed with a teddy bear on it, nightstand with an empty tissue box. Towel, mud mask, corsage, phone.

LIGHTS UP on EMMA'S bedroom. EMMA stands with her back to the audience, wearing a robe with a towel wrapped around her hair and a mud mask on her face. DEREK stands to the side and "knocks" on her bedroom door.

DEREK: Hello! Knock, knock! Can I come in?

EMMA: *(Turns around and we see her mud mask.)* Come in.

DEREK: *(Mimes opening a door. ENTERS.)* Whoa!

EMMA: Did you come to wish me good luck?

DEREK: You aren't ready? You look...!

EMMA: I know, I know. But don't worry. This will all come together soon. It's a process. *(Smiles.)* I still can't believe it. This is a dream come true for me!

DEREK: My big sister! Nominated for homecoming queen! *(As if presenting her.)* Here's the winner! Right here!

EMMA: Oh, thank you. *(Waves and blows kisses.)* Thank you, thank you, thank you. *(To DEREK.)* How was that? I've been practicing.

DEREK: That's great. But...

EMMA: What?

DEREK: What are you going to do if you don't win? I mean—don't get me wrong—I know it's highly unlikely, but what if they don't call your name?

EMMA: Wow. I hadn't thought about that. I can't look disappointed... or worse, cry!

DEREK: No. You've got to come across as a gracious loser.

EMMA: You're right. I suppose I should practice this. Let's pretend you're the winner.

DEREK: *(Takes a step forward and announces in a deep voice.)* "And this year's homecoming queen is... Derek Doolittle!" *(EMMA smiles and claps. DEREK steps back and covers his mouth. In a falsetto.)* Me? Me? Oh, my gosh! I can't believe it!

EMMA: *(Throws her arms around him.)* Congratulations! I'm so happy for you!

DEREK: Thank you! Thank you! Oh, thank you! *(Waves and blows kisses, and then prompts EMMA.)* I need my crown!

EMMA: Oh! Oh! Hold on. *(Grabs an empty tissue box and places it on his head.)*

DEREK: Uh, flowers. I need flowers too.

EMMA: Oh, yeah. *(Grabs a teddy bear and hands it to him.)*

DEREK: *(Smiles.)* I feel so honored! *(Prompts.)* Now, you need to take my picture for the newspaper.

EMMA: *(Pretends to take his picture.)* Click, click. Click, click. As the audience cheers and claps.

DEREK: *(Enjoys the moment, prompts.)* Congratulate me again. Just for extra practice.

EMMA: Congratulations, Derek! I knew you'd win! You deserve it.

DEREK: I kind of like this. Thank you! Thank you! *(Blows a kiss.)*

EMMA: *(Knocks the crown off.)* Okay, that's enough. You've got the winning part down, and I've practiced becoming a gracious loser.

DEREK: You're going to win, sis. I even had a dream that you won.

EMMA: You did? Well, I hope that dreams come true.

DEREK: You're about to find out. Your escort is right outside the door.

EMMA: Brandon's here? But how can that be? I still have hours to get ready.

DEREK: I don't know, but he's outside that door with a mum for you to wear. And that thing is huge! I swear, those mums get bigger every year.

EMMA: You're lying!

DEREK: No, I'm not! They get bigger every year. I don't know how you girls can wear one. They're so heavy! Must take a hundred pins to keep it on. Like carrying a backpack in front. And I bet by the time you take it off, your back is killing you. *(Puts his hand on his back.)* Oh, my aching back! I've been carrying around this huge mum all day!

EMMA: Brandon isn't here! He can't be outside the door! You're lying!

DEREK: No, I'm not. He's right outside the door. I promise.

EMMA: *(Goes to the door, opens it, slams it, and screams.)* What is he doing here?!

DEREK: He's here to escort you to the game. Then, at half time, you'll go to the center of the football field with the other nominees and wait anxiously as they call out the winner. "And the homecoming queen is…" And everyone screams and cheers.

EMMA: *(Panics.)* What time is it?

DEREK: Six o'clock. Aren't you supposed to be at the football field by six thirty?

EMMA: *(Screams.)* It can't be six! I still have hours to get ready!

DEREK: *(Looks at his phone.)* No, I'd say you have five minutes.

EMMA: Let me see that! *(Looks at his phone and screams.)* Is this a bad dream? Tell me it's a bad dream! Tell me!

DEREK: No, but do you want me to slap you in the face?

EMMA: Yes! I mean, no! I mean, wake me up already! *(The door opens, and BRANDON ENTERS with a corsage.)*

BRANDON: What's going on? Are you ready? *(Looks at her.)* Hey, why aren't you ready? We need to leave.

EMMA: What are you doing in here?!

BRANDON: I came to pick you up.

EMMA: But I'm not ready!

DEREK: *(Tries to be helpful.)* She's not ready. You know how girls are. They like to spend hours and hours in front of the mirror. *(Looks at his phone.)* But, Emma, you're running out of time.

BRANDON: Why aren't you ready?

EMMA: I have hours to get ready! To paint my toes, deep condition my hair—which I'm doing right now—wash my hair, dry my hair, curl my hair, put on makeup, slip into my new dress, and twirl in front of the mirror at least a million times! And take selfies! And take some family pictures with Mom and Dad. And check the mirror again, and add more hairspray, and another selfie... So, I just want to know— why are you here so early?!

BRANDON: I'm here to pick you up! Let's go. *(EMMA screams. The door opens, and MOM and DAD ENTER.)*

MOM: Honey, are you ready? Dad and I wanted to take some family pictures before you leave. *(Acts as if EMMA looks fine.)* Derek, would you take our picture together?

DAD: Honey, you look beautiful. Even if you don't win tonight, you know your mom and I are very proud of you.

EMMA: Dad! *(MOM and DAD pose beside her, as DEREK pulls out his phone to take their picture.)*

DEREK: Okay, on the count of three, smile. One, two, three! *(MOM and DAD smile as EMMA panics.)*

EMMA: This can't be happening! I need to wake up!

BRANDON: Are you ready to go?

EMMA: Do I look like I'm ready to go?!

MOM: You look fine, dear.

DAD: You always look beautiful to me. My little princess.

DEREK: She doesn't look ready to me, but I'm sure that your robe will be fine. And I'm sure no one will notice your lack of makeup. Or that towel on your head. It sort of looks like a crown. But you might want to throw on some slippers or something. You don't want to walk out on the field barefooted. Now that would be embarrassing!

EMMA: I'm not going like this!

MOM: Honey, you look fine. Just go as you are. I don't want you to be late.

EMMA: Are you serious? Stand on the football field in front of thousands of spectators wearing my bathrobe? While the other nominees are wearing adorable dresses? You want me to go and look like this? Like this?!

MOM: I don't want you to be late.

DAD: You look beautiful, sweetheart.

EMMA: *(Desperate.)* Dad! Mom!

DEREK: You look great, Emma. Go. Go! Don't be late to homecoming!

BRANDON: Come on! Let's go! *(DAD opens the door.)*

DEREK: Good luck, sis. I hope you win. Don't forget to wave and show them your killer smile. *(Waves.)* Thank you, thank you, thank you. *(Takes BRANDON'S arm and pulls him out the door. They EXIT.)*

MOM: Oh, honey, I'm so proud of you. You're a winner to your dad and me no matter what happens on the field tonight.

DAD: Yes, so proud! *(EXITS with MOM and shuts the door. EMMA collapses on the bed and then sits up, yawning.)*

EMMA: Wow. What a nightmare! That'll teach me not to take a nap.

DEREK: *(Knocks and ENTERS.)* Hey... *(Notices her.)* Whoa! You're not ready yet?

EMMA: *(Starts to panic.)* Why? What time is it? What time is it?!

DEREK: Hey, relax. It's only two. You still have hours to get ready.

EMMA: *(Sighs, relieved, and then remembers.)* Oh, I have so much to do! I've got to get ready! *(Rushes OFF.)*

DEREK: *(Calls OFF.)* Don't forget to practice smiling and waving. *(Grabs the tissue box and puts it on his head, then smiles and waves.)* Thank you! Oh, thank you! *(LIGHTS FADE to BLACK.)*

WEDDING PLANS

CAST OF CHARACTERS

MILA (F) .... controlling girlfriend
ANNA (F) .... her friend
NAIL TECH ONE (M) .... manicurist
NAIL TECH TWO (M) .... another

SETTING
A nail salon.

PROPERTIES
Two manicure tables, four chairs. Manicure tools, two bottles of nail polish, two small dishes of water, two cell phones, box of tissues.

LIGHTS UP on MILA and ANNA getting manicures at a nail salon. NAIL TECH ONE sits in front of MILA, and NAIL TECH TWO sits in front of ANNA.

MILA: So, anyway, I told Joey that if I didn't have a ring on my finger by Valentine's Day, it was over.

ANNA: Just like that?

MILA: *(Snaps.)* Just like that.

TECH ONE: *(Finishes arranging his tools.)* What are we having today, ladies?

MILA: The deluxe manicures.

TECH TWO: Did you pick your color?

ANNA: Yes. Here's mine. *(Hands her nail polish to TECH TWO.)*

TECH TWO: Good choice. Pretty color.

ANNA: Thank you.

MILA: *(Hands polish to TECH ONE.)* Here's mine. *(To ANNA.)* Oh! And I've already picked out my dress. Oh, my gosh! Wait until you see it! It's gorgeous!

ANNA: Wow! That's exciting. You just need the ring now.

MILA: Yes. Soon. Very soon!

ANNA: I told Charles that we needed to date at least another year, then we'd see. See how it goes. See if I still like him. See if I'm sure. You know?

MILA: Of course, you'll still like him. You're being overly cautious.

ANNA: Maybe, but what's the rush?

MILA: After one year, you should know. And I know. So now it's up to me.

ANNA: What do you mean?

MILA: Men are slow. They need hints. Direction. Ultimatums.

TECH ONE: Ultimatums? Oh, no! Don't do that.

MILA: Why? What's wrong with ultimatums?

TECH ONE: Here, soak your fingers in this water. Men don't like pressure. They don't want to be told they must do this or that or you're leaving them. Let a man be a man and make his own decisions.

TECH TWO: Preach it, brother.

TECH ONE: My ex-girlfriend did that to me when I was considering leaving professional football to pursue my passion.

MILA: What was your passion?

TECH ONE: *(Lifts her hand and inspects her nails.)* Creating beautiful nails for beautiful women.

MILA/ANNA: Aw...

TECH TWO: But his girlfriend didn't approve and gave him an ultimatum.

TECH ONE: *(Falsetto.)* "Either you keep playing football and making lots of money and taking me where there are lots of cameras and celebrities, or it's over!"

MILA: So she left you?

TECH ONE: Yes. But that's okay, because I'm happy now. I, ex-boyfriend and ex-professional football player, am the best nail technician in this state. *(Inspects her hand.)* Wow. We've got a lot of work to do here.

MILA: Well, my relationship with Joey is completely different. He needs direction.

ANNA: Valentine's Day or it's over?

MILA: Exactly. Did I tell you I picked out my colors?

ANNA: No. What are they?

MILA: Purple, burgundy, and orange.

ANNA: *(Unsure.)* Wow. That sounds... colorful.

MILA: Yes. Deep, moody, and romantic.

ANNA: Moody is a good description. How many bridesmaids do you plan on having?

MILA: Eight.

ANNA: Eight? Wow. That's a huge wedding. I hate to ask, but am I...?

MILA: And... I've picked the date too!

ANNA: Already? Before you even have the ring?

MILA: What can I say? I'm a planner.

ANNA: Indeed. So, eight bridesmaids...

MILA: At least. Do you think it would be too much to have ten? Or maybe twelve?

TECH TWO: Overkill!

MILA: Excuse me?

TECH TWO: Sorry. I know you didn't ask for my opinion. That just slipped out.

MILA: It's okay. I don't want to overdo it. I just want the perfect wedding. You know, like you see in the magazines. What are your thoughts, Anna?

ANNA: Ten to twelve bridesmaids? Hmm... I think I'd stick with eight. Or less.

MILA: I think you're right. And yes, Anna. You're one of them.

ANNA: Oh, good!

MILA: *(To TECH ONE.)* Work your magic, because my nails must look pretty when I show off my huge diamond ring.

TECH ONE: And beautiful nails you shall have, give or take a ring.

MILA: What's that supposed to mean?

TECH TWO: He meant that even when you drop the football, the game is still on. So, even if you don't get the ring, life goes on.

TECH ONE: Yeah! That's what I meant.

ANNA: *(To TECH TWO.)* Did you play football too?

TECH TWO: I did. Then I injured my back and followed my buddy over here into this new career. Beautiful nails for beautiful women.

MILA/ANNA: Aw...

TECH TWO: Now, let's soften up these beautiful hands.

ANNA: Thank you! *(To MILA.)* Did you hear that? I have beautiful hands.

MILA: I heard that. *(To TECH ONE.)* Ouch! What are you doing?

TECH ONE: Getting that nastiness out from under your nails.

MILA: Nastiness?

TECH ONE: Have you been digging in the dirt?

MILA: No!

TECH TWO: *(Holds up polish.)* Yes. Very pretty color.

ANNA: Thank you! *(To MILA.)* He likes my color.

MILA: I think he said that earlier. *(To TECH ONE.)* Do you like my color?

TECH ONE: Truthfully?

MILA: Does that mean you're going to say no?

TECH ONE: If you like it, I like it.

MILA: Well, I like it! *(To ANNA.)* So, anyway, back to my wedding. I told Joey that he better buy me a good size ring. Huge. Enormous. A ring to make everyone envious. In awe. Jealous. Yes, jealous. *(Smiles and looks at her hand.)*

ANNA: But Mila, Joey's not exactly loaded. He's like Charles. Barely enough for rent.

MILA: Credit card!

ANNA: Do you think that's wise?

TECH ONE: I don't.

TECH TWO: Me neither.

MILA: What is it with you male technicians? Do you have to be so nosey?

TECH TWO: We are often asked for our opinions. Acrylic or gel? Pink or red? Do I need to wax my upper lip? Usually the answer is yes. Where's a good place to eat around here? Are you on Facebook? Can I add you as my friend? Should I expect my boyfriend to charge a humongous engagement ring to his credit card? You know, stuff like that.

MILA: But I didn't ask for your opinion, did I?

TECH TWO: Pardon me.

TECH ONE: Look at all the dead skin around your cuticles. Nasty.

MILA: Would you please quit calling my nails nasty.

TECH ONE: We'll get you beautiful soon. Trust me.

MILA: *(To ANNA.)* So, anyway, I told Joey that the size of a ring shows everyone how much he loves me. Either a little or more than anyone can imagine! *(To TECH ONE.)* Ouch! That hurt! *(To ANNA.)* Anyway, I better get a huge rock on my hand!

TECH ONE: Or what?

MILA: Or what? You're asking me, "Or what?" Get back to making me beautiful. Please!

ANNA: Then I'll ask. Or what?

MILA: Well, there is no "or what," because I get what I want! And I want a rock! Ouch! You're going to make me bleed with those little cutters!

TECH TWO: *(Rubs oil on ANNA'S cuticles. To ANNA.)* Feel nice?

ANNA: *(To TECH TWO.)* Yes, so relaxing. I love that oil you massage into my cuticles.

MILA: So, anyway, do you want to host my bridal shower? I already have the date.

ANNA: Sure, but…

MILA: *(Pulls out her phone.)* I've also started choosing my selections on Amazon. Of course, it's not live yet. I'm just waiting for my proposal next Thursday.

ANNA: Mila, are you sure he's going to ask you to marry him?

MILA: Of course, I'm sure. Valentine's Day. I told Joey I would be available between six and eight p.m. for our romantic evening together. Then afterwards, I need time to post pics of my ring on social media and update my status. Engaged!

ANNA: You're pushing Joey aside at eight p.m. so you can post on social media?

MILA: Well, yeah! I need to let everyone know what's going on. Oh, I can't wait to see how many likes I get. Hundreds, I'm sure. *(To TECH ONE.)* Hey! Can you paint some little hearts on my fingers too?

TECH ONE: Maybe I should paint a question mark. Maybe he'll ask, maybe he won't. *(TECH TWO and ANNA laugh. MILA glares at ANNA.)*

ANNA: I'm sorry. I'm trying not to laugh, but that was funny.

TECH ONE: Maybe so. Maybe no.

TECH TWO: You want hearts on your fingernails? Maybe just a couple of small ones?

ANNA: Oh, yes! Please. Valentine's Day is next week.

MILA: *(To ANNA.)* You got the nice technician. I got the hateful one!

TECH TWO: Then pretty hearts it will be.

ANNA: *(Smiles.)* Thank you!

MILA: So, anyway, Thursday between six and eight p.m. is the designated time.

ANNA: Mila, aren't you a little disappointed that it's not going to be a big surprise? You know, you're out for a romantic moonlit walk when suddenly—when you least expect it—he drops to one knee and...

MILA: That's what I forgot!

ANNA: What?

MILA: I've got to text Joey! *(Texts with one hand.)* Don't forget to drop to one knee! Sent.

ANNA: Wow. You plan every detail, don't you?

MILA: *(Texts more.)* And say...

ANNA: You're telling him what to say?

TECH ONE: I've heard it all now.

MILA: *(To TECH ONE.)* You stay out of this.

TECH ONE: It's hard to do your nails when you're texting.

MILA: Give me a sec. *(Texts with both hands.)* "How I love thee, let me count the ways. I love thee to the depth and breadth and height..."

ANNA: Mila, that doesn't really sound like Joey. I mean to quote a sonnet...

MILA: Maybe I'll take that part off. Maybe it was too much. But he can say this... *(Texts.)*

TECH ONE: Can't he just speak from his heart?

MILA: *(Ignores him. Texts.)* "I can't live my life without you! Here I am, down on my knee, begging you—yes!—begging you..."

TECH TWO: He has to beg?

TECH ONE: *(Begs like a dog.)* Arf! Arf! Arf!

119

MILA: Stop that!

ANNA: You know, begging doesn't sound like something Joey would do either.

MILA: Fine! Then I'll rewrite my proposal!

TECH ONE: Or let your boyfriend write it himself. Yes, thank you! Genius advice here.

TECH TWO: *(Claps.)* Great advice! *(Speaks into an imaginary microphone.)* So, tell us, how did you come across this unbelievable, lifesaving advice for this confused and desperate wife-to-be?

TECH ONE: Well, it's called common sense. Common sense with a capital C!

MILA: I'm not laughing. Do you see me laughing? I know you two ex-football players don't get it, but I need to tell Joey what to say so he won't mess this up. Otherwise, he'd probably say, "Hey, you want to get hitched, or what?"

ANNA: That sounds more like the Joey I know.

TECH ONE: Sounds good to me.

TECH TWO: Nothing wrong with that.

MILA: Well, that's not acceptable! So, I'll tell him what to say. *(Texts.)* "My love, I would be honored if you would agree to become my wife. Your beauty, your dynamic personality, your wisdom, your beauty..."

TECH TWO: You already said beauty.

MILA: *(Glares. Texts.)* "Your beauty, your love is all that I desire in this entire world. So, please, oh please..."

TECH ONE: Please make her stop.

MILA: "Please, will you marry me?" Sent. How was that?

TECH ONE: Truthfully?

MILA: I wasn't asking you! Paint my nails. *(Forces a smile.)* Please.

TECH TWO: Man, I wouldn't have sent that.

MILA: I already sent it! What is it with you guys? You aren't here to meddle in my life. Just give us manicures. *(Turns to ANNA.)* Well? What do you think?

ANNA: Well, I... I...

TECH ONE: She thinks it's dumb too.

MILA: Don't speak for her! In fact, don't speak at all! *(To ANNA.)* Well?

ANNA: Well, I think you should let him come up with his own proposal.

MILA: Well, it's too late! I already sent it. I'm sure he's memorizing it as we speak.

ANNA: Maybe.

MILA: *(Holds up her phone.)* Do you want to see a picture of my dress? Oh, wait. Joey just sent me a text.

TECH ONE: You need to put that down and let the base dry. Hand it to me, and I'll read it for you.

MILA: Fine. Then read it to me. *(Hands him the phone.)* What did he say?

TECH ONE: *(Reads.)* "I can't do this."

MILA: What?!

ANNA: Uh-oh. I think Joey's getting cold feet.

TECH ONE: Or getting smart.

MILA: I can't believe this! He's backing out?

ANNA: I'm sorry, Mila. You'll be okay.

MILA: Well, of course, I'll be okay! But how can he do this to me?

ANNA: Maybe it's just too much too soon. *(Looks at her phone.)* I just got a text from Charles.

MILA: What did he say? *(Scoots ANNA'S phone towards TECH TWO.)* Can you please read it for me so I don't mess up my nails?

TECH TWO: Sure. *(Reads.)* "In case I've never told you, I'm so lucky to have you in my life." Aw. Sweet. Oh, and he wants to know if you're free for dinner.

MILA: *(To TECH ONE.)* Text Joey back for me. Say this, "Fine with me!"

TECH ONE: *(Texts.)* Done.

TECH TWO: *(To ANNA.)* You got another text.

ANNA: What does it say?

TECH TWO: Dinner on Valentine's Day. You and me. Something special. Something you'll never forget!

ANNA: Oh, my gosh! I think… I think this proposal talk has rubbed off on Charles!

MILA: *(Uninterested. To TECH ONE.)* Text Joey again. Say this, "In fact, I'm relieved it's off. No more stressing over details."

TECH ONE: Whatever you want to say. *(Texts.)* Sent.

ANNA: And now... I don't know... I'm suddenly excited! I think Charles is going to propose to me on Valentine's Day!

TECH TWO: I think you might be right. I'm happy for you.

ANNA: Thank you!

TECH ONE: *(To MILA.)* He sent another text.

MILA: What did he say? Hurry! Tell me what he said!

TECH ONE: That last text was for Charles, not you. Sorry. I'm helping him pick out an engagement ring for Anna. I'm not good at this stuff.

ANNA: An engagement ring for me? *(Screams with excitement. MILA begins to cry.)*

TECH TWO: Uh-oh. I have some tissues. Want one?

TECH ONE: And another text from Joey.

MILA: *(Between sobs.)* I don't care!

TECH ONE: *(Reads.)* So, if you don't mind picking out your own ring, that'd be great.

MILA: What? What? Pick out my own ring?

TECH ONE: That's what he said.

MILA: *(Screams.)* Yes! I'm getting my proposal!

ANNA: Me too! *(BOTH scream.)*

TECH ONE: Another text from Joey. "But nothing too big because I can't afford it." *(MILA begins crying again. TECH TWO hands her the tissues. LIGHTS FADE to BLACK.)*

———○———

THE DEATH OF ANTS

CAST OF CHARACTERS

BRIDGET (F)... college girl
JOSH (M)... young nice guy

SETTING
A downtown sidewalk.

PROPERTIES
Bench. Tissue.

LIGHTS UP on BRIDGET shuffling down a sidewalk, depressed. She notices a bench and sits down.

BRIDGET: *(Muses to herself.)* I need a dog. Or a cat. Or a fish. Yeah, it'd be nice if someone would listen to me. *(Looks at the ground.)* Oh, there's an ant. Hello, little ant. Mind if I talk to you? Great. I have an ant to talk to. Guess it beats nothing—or rather, no one. So here's the deal, little ant. I hate my life. Yeah. That pretty much sums it up. Why, you might ask? Are you ready for this? For one thing, I crashed into a parked car. Bam! No, I wasn't texting and driving. I was crying. The tears in my eyes had me seeing all blurry. Why was I crying, you might ask? Well, let me back up. First, I was late for work. I overslept, okay? Then, when I showed up at work, my boss let me have it. *(Yells.)* "Do you see what time it is? It's 12:05! You are one hour and five minutes late, missy!" *(Quieter.)* What was I supposed to say? I overslept? Uh, I don't think so. So I lied. "Mr. Sid, I was having car problems. My car wouldn't start." Now, Mr. Ant, that's karma right there, because you and I both know that was a big fat lie. Yeah, I lied. And Mr. Sid kept screaming. "I have a business to run here! You irresponsible college kids are not worth the money I pay you! Showing up late! Always on your phones! Whining about life! I've just about had it with all of you!" And what do I do, Mr.

Ant? Well, I dip a scoop of black raspberry crunch ice cream and plop it on his bald head. Oh, and I didn't stop there! I grabbed the whip cream and sprinkles and finished off my delicious creation. "Take that!" I said. "And by the way... I quit!" Then, I raced to my car and drove off like a maniac. And you know what, little ant? I needed that job. I have bills to pay. I'm a college student trying to make ends meet. But who's going to hire me now? So, I'm driving down the street, balling like a baby, and that's when I rammed into a parked car. *(Waits for a reaction.)* Did you hear me? I ran into a parked car. Parked. *(Pause.)* Are you listening to me? Anyway, I don't have collision insurance, so I'm out of luck. What could I do but walk home? Sure, I have a thumb, but that's not safe. So I'm walking, walking down the street, when I realized I left my house keys in my car. Which is at the repair shop about five miles back there. So, I'm wondering, what can possibly go wrong next? Hey! Are you listening to me? Why are you running away from me? Stop! Stop! *(Stands and jumps in front of the ant. JOSH ENTERS and watches her.)* Can you stop and listen to me? Please! *(Listens.)* Oh, yeah? Well, fine! *(Stomps on the ant.)* Take that! *(Continues to stomp.)* And that! And that!

JOSH: Wow. You must have myrmecophobia.

BRIDGET: *(Quickly turns.)* What? What did you say I have?

JOSH: I said, you must have myrmecophobia.

BRIDGET: Do I look like I have... whatever it was that you just said you think I have?

JOSH: Yes. *(Mimics her, including the stomping.)* Take that! And that! And that!

BRIDGET: That's fine. Go ahead and make fun of me. I'll add that to my list. "Was made fun of today by a complete stranger." Check. Now if you don't mind, can you explain my diagnosis?

JOSH: It's a phobia. An overwhelming and unreasonable fear of ants. In reality, he... *(Points.)* ...the ant, poses no real danger, but to you, it provokes anxiety, avoidance, and apparently violent reactions. Poor little guy.

BRIDGET: The ant?

JOSH: *(Points.)* Oh, look. There's another one. Are you going to kill that one too?

BRIDGET: After the day I've had, you bet I am! *(Stomps on the ant.)* Oh, and there's another one! And another! *(Angrily stomps them all.)* Take that! And that! And that!

JOSH: Wow. You do have a severe case of myrmecophobia. Look, they're small. Innocent. They don't want to kill you like you want to kill them.

BRIDGET: Look, I've had a bad day. You're making it worse!

JOSH: Me? Josh here, who everyone thinks is a super nice guy?

BRIDGET: Yes, you! *(Points.)* That ant... he used to be my friend. Well, until...

JOSH: Your friend?

BRIDGET: I needed someone to talk to, okay? But then he started running away. So I... you know...

JOSH: So, you don't have a fear of ants?

BRIDGET: No. I'll even prove it to you. *(Reaches down to let an ant climb on her hand.)* See. I'm holding this one. Hello, little ant. *(Watches it and starts to breathe heavy.)* But I can't say I especially like holding it. And I'm starting to feel... I don't know... like I can't breathe... its little legs crawling on my skin... I hope it doesn't bite me. Please don't bite me. Oh! It's crawling up my arm. I think it wants to crawl all over my body. On my face. In my nose... *(Gasps for air.)* I can't do this! Get off me! Get off me! *(Flings the ant off and stomps on it. Looks at JOSH.)* Don't say it.

JOSH: What? That perhaps you do have myrmecophobia?

BRIDGET: But I don't. It's just... He wanted to eat me alive!

JOSH: Relax. Not all phobias need treatment. But if it affects your daily life, you might want to seek professional help.

BRIDGET: *(Glares at him.)* Who are you? And why are you invading my terrible day and making it worse?

JOSH: *(Offers his hand, but she refuses.)* Josh Dawson. And I apologize. I was enjoying some fresh air on this warm, sunny day, when I noticed you murdering that ant. So, you're having a terrible day?

BRIDGET: Yes. May I borrow your phone? I need to call a friend to rescue me. Not that I have a lot of friends. A couple. But then again... Monica is in Jamaica with her parents. And Cameron is having his appendix removed as we speak. Then there's my ex-boyfriend who I'm not speaking to. My parents live two hundred fifty miles away. My boss fired me. No. I quit. I quit before he could fire me. So, who can I call?

JOSH: Ghostbusters? Sorry. Bad joke. Sorry, but I left my phone on my desk. *(Points across the street.)* But it's just over there. Across the street. That's where I...

BRIDGET: Figures! But who would I call, anyway? My dog? Oh, wait. I don't have a dog. Or a cat. Or a fish. I guess that's why I was talking to an ant.

JOSH: And he wouldn't listen to you?

BRIDGET: No, he wouldn't! So, I... *(Stomps.)* ...killed him. And that one also. *(Stomps her foot.)* And that one. And that one...

JOSH: Whoa! Whoa! Hold on. Calm down.

BRIDGET: Stupid ants.

JOSH: You know, I have two ears. *(Points.)* One. Two.

BRIDGET: Your point?

JOSH: I could be your friend. As long as you don't, you know...

BRIDGET: What? Kill you? Do I look like I'm going to kill someone?

JOSH: You did. And yes.

BRIDGET: Well, I'm not! *(Stomps.)* Just stupid ants, that's all. I kind of like killing them, you know?

JOSH: I see that. So, anyway, do you want to talk to me? Josh Dawson, friendliest person on Earth.

BRIDGET: Friendly or not, I don't know you.

JOSH: I'm Josh. We just met. What did you say your name was?

BRIDGET: I didn't. *(Pause.)* Bridget.

JOSH: Hi, Bridget. So, allow me to assist you by pretending to be your friend. I'm better than an ant, aren't I?

BRIDGET: Are you going to run away too?

JOSH: Only if I feel as if my life is being threatened.

BRIDGET: Funny. Very funny. Okay. I'll take you up on your offer.

JOSH: So, spill it.

BRIDGET: Spill it?

JOSH: Your guts.

BRIDGET: Okay... I hate my life.

JOSH: That's dramatic. Go on.

BRIDGET: Last night, I broke up with my boyfriend.

JOSH: Of course, the boyfriend crisis. Now you feel desperate and unloved and unsure about the world as a single person. And you feel as if you'll be single for the rest of your life now? You'll never love another, and another will never love you? Bridget, it takes time. What you need to do is cry. Feel the emotions. Don't hold them in. So, go ahead. Cry. *(Pulls out a tissue from his pocket.)* Tissue?

BRIDGET: No! I don't want to cry! I was crying all night.

JOSH: Good, good.

BRIDGET: Which is why I was late to work. My boss chewed me out, so I threw black raspberry crunch ice cream on his bald head with whipped cream and sprinkles! And before he could fire me, I quit. Dang, I needed that job.

JOSH: Jobs are a dime a dozen. Well, I take that back. Not in this economy. You might be sorry you did that, but then again, it sounds like you were about to be fired, so that was probably a smart move.

BRIDGET: And then... are you ready for this?

JOSH: Hit me.

BRIDGET: I left work crying and what did I do? I drove into a parked car. *(Raises hand.)* Guilty! My fault!

JOSH: Ticket?

BRIDGET: Well, of course, I got a ticket! Then the tow truck people haul my car off, and... *(Waves.)* Bye! I'm car-less. My phone is dead, so I start walking home. Five miles later, it hits me. My house keys are in the car!

JOSH: Dang!

BRIDGET: Told ya! See why I hate my life?

JOSH: Bridget, cars can be repaired. You'll find another job and a new boyfriend.

BRIDGET: Stop!

JOSH: It gets worse?

BRIDGET: Worse? How could it get worse? I'm single, unemployed, and practically homeless. And my phone is dead!

JOSH: Don't leave out ant-killer. Poor little guy. Make that "guys." You killed a lot of them. If you hadn't, they'd still be crawling along that little trail in hopes of finding a dead insect or breadcrumb to eat, enjoying the warm summer day... *(Deep, sad breath.)*

BRIDGET: Great! Now I'm a single, unemployed, homeless, ant-killer!

JOSH: Dang. Maybe I should run for it.

BRIDGET: I wouldn't blame you. That's what they did.

JOSH: So... is there more?

BRIDGET: More?

JOSH: More bad stuff?

BRIDGET: I don't know, Josh, because the day hasn't ended yet! I'm sure there could be more!

JOSH: I know. Let's think of something positive and turn this day around for you. Okay. We need ideas. Ideas... Do you have any ideas?

BRIDGET: *(Sits down on bench.)* Yeah. I could sit here and murder ants as they crawl past my feet. At least I'd feel powerful, in a murderous type of way.

JOSH: *(Sits next to her.)* Question. Do you mind getting a ride home in a hearse?

BRIDGET: A hearse? Like where they put dead people?

JOSH: That's the one. I work at the funeral home across the street, and that's the only vehicle available at the moment. Would you believe my car is in the shop too? Alternator is out. But I could give you a ride to the body shop to get your keys, then to your place. That is, if you don't mind riding in a hearse. There is a body in the back, but he won't bother us. He's headed to Sunset Memorial later this afternoon for a little graveside party.

BRIDGET: Well, I guess I don't mind. If you're sure you don't mind.

JOSH: Not at all. I have time. Hey, I bet you like being around dead bodies, don't you?

BRIDGET: Excuse me?

JOSH: I mean, death obviously doesn't bother you. Does it?

BRIDGET: *(Stomps on an ant.)* Apparently not.

JOSH: Well, the funeral home is looking for a greeter. You know, to make families feel welcome during their time of sorrow. I think you'd be perfect.

BRIDGET: Comfort and welcome people? I could do that. *(Takes JOSH'S hand and demonstrates.)* We're so sorry for your loss. Please let me know if there's anything you need— anything at all. Coffee? Tea? *(Offers him the tissue.)* Tissue?

JOSH: That's great! So, if you'd like me to, I can put in a good word for you, which means... *(Shakes her hand.)* Congratulations. You've got the job.

BRIDGET: Already?

JOSH: Yep. *(Smiles.)* My dad's the owner.

BRIDGET: This is wonderful!

JOSH: Oh, and one more thing.

BRIDGET: Yeah?

JOSH: Since you broke up with your boyfriend, do you want to go out on Friday? You know, just as a pretend boyfriend.

BRIDGET: Uh...

JOSH: Come on. Say yes.

BRIDGET: Yes.

JOSH: *(Stands.)* Great! Come on. Let's go get the black tuxedo.

BRIDGET: *(Stands.)* The black tuxedo?

JOSH: Hearse. Sometimes we call it that.

BRIDGET: There really is a dead body in the back?

JOSH: Yeah. Just another day at the office.

BRIDGET: Thanks, Josh.

JOSH: No problem.

BRIDGET: Guess I don't hate my life after all. But, you know... *(Stomps.)* ...I still don't like ants.

JOSH: Yeah. Glad I'm not an ant.

BRIDGET: You should be! *(They laugh and EXIT. LIGHTS FADE to BLACK.)*

THE EYE EXAM

CAST OF CHARACTERS

DYLAN (M) ....nearsighted teen
ALEX (E) .... his friend who wears glasses
RECEPTIONIST (E) .... smart skeptic
DOCTOR (E) ....no fool

SETTING
An optometrist's office.

PROPERTIES
Receptionist desk, four chairs, stool, small desk. Clipboard with paper, pen, flashlight pen, stylish glasses, hand mirror.

LIGHTS UP on the RECEPTIONIST, sitting behind the desk. Three or four chairs are lined up LEFT to create the waiting room. A receptionist's desk and chair are UP CENTER. The RIGHT side of the stage is the exam room, where there is a stool and a small desk. DYLAN ENTERS LEFT, followed by ALEX, who wears glasses.

DYLAN: Thanks for driving me here. Mom had some emergency come up at work.

ALEX: No problem, my friend.

DYLAN: This actually works better for me, because I have a plan.

ALEX: A plan for what?

DYLAN: For passing my eye exam!

ALEX: How are you going to do that? It's not like you can study for an eye exam.

DYLAN: Oh, but I did! I, Dylan Smith, found the standard eye chart used by most optometrists, and... I studied it. Or, let's say, memorized it.

ALEX: Are you crazy?

DYLAN: Look, I don't want to wear glasses! Can you see this face—this face right here—wearing glasses?

ALEX: *(Pushes up his glasses.)* I wear them. What's wrong with them?

DYLAN: Well, you look great in glasses! Smart. Honest. Trustworthy. But they're not for me. Not for this face.

ALEX: But if you need glasses—

DYLAN: I don't need them. Trust me. I can see just fine without them. I better go check in.

ALEX: I'm gonna go sit down. *(Sits in the waiting area.)*

DYLAN: *(Crosses to the RECEPTIONIST.)* Hi, I have an appointment at three.

RECEPTIONIST: Name?

DYLAN: Dylan Smith.

RECEPTIONIST: *(Hands him a clipboard and pen.)* Fill this out, please.

DYLAN: Okay, thanks. *(Takes the clipboard and runs into a chair as he goes to sit down.)*

ALEX: You okay?

DYLAN: I'm fine. Clumsy me. *(Sits next to ALEX and holds the paper closer and closer to his face, trying to read the questions. He slowly writes down the answers.)*

ALEX: Dylan, listen to me. You can't fake your eye exam.

DYLAN: Want to bet? *(Pretends to read a chart on the wall.)* E-F-P-T-O-Z—

ALEX: It gets smaller.

DYLAN: I got this. L-P-E-D. Next line, P-E-C-F-O. Next line, E-D-F-C-Z-P. *(Squints.)* The last line... Let's see. Barely, yes, barely, I can see it. P-E-Z-O-L-C-F-T-I. That'll impress the doctor. I doubt many people can read that last line.

ALEX: Wow! How did you memorize all that?

DYLAN: It wasn't easy, believe me! I had to make up this little jingle. *(Sings.)* L-P-E-D... P-E-C-F-O...

ALEX: Wow, I'm truly impressed.

DYLAN: Going to ace this exam! Because I refuse, absolutely refuse, to put glasses on this face! *(Points to his face, then makes a few dramatic poses.)* This is model material here.

ALEX: Hey, models wear glasses.

DYLAN: Not this one!

ALEX: But you'd look great. Not to mention being able to see.

DYLAN: Nope. Nope, nope, nope. I'm not going to do it.

ALEX: There's always contacts.

DYLAN: And put those huge saucers in my eyes? No way! I couldn't do that.

ALEX: Oh, come on. They're not that big. They're small.

DYLAN: Then why don't you wear them?

ALEX: I actually like the way I look in glasses.

DYLAN: And you look great in them! But me, I can't see myself in them. No pun intended. *(Finishes the paperwork and stands.)* Like I said, I see just fine. *(Runs into another chair as he crosses to the RECEPTIONIST. Hands her the clipboard and pen.)*

RECEPTIONIST: Thank you. We'll be with you in a few minutes. *(DYLAN sits down.)*

ALEX: So, tell me, how did you get that eye chart?

DYLAN: Online. It's the standard one that all the eye doctors use. Yep, I'm going to ace this exam. L-P-E-D. P-E-C-F-O.

ALEX: Dylan, glasses can be awesome. They have all these cool styles and colors to choose from. They can even enhance your personality.

DYLAN: My personality shines already without spectacles disrupting my look. *(Strikes a pose.)*

ALEX: You may need to lose that attitude and accept your fate.

DYLAN: My fate is to be me. This. As you see me now.

ALEX: I see you, but how well can you see me? That's the question.

DYLAN: To be or not to be? That is the question. To be without glasses is my answer. L-P-E-D. P-E-C-F-O. I'll really impress the doctor when I blast off the last line. I'll act like I can barely see it so he'll believe it's real.

ALEX: I don't support this, Dylan.

RECEPTIONIST: Dylan Smith, the doctor will see you now. *(DYLAN follows the RECEPTIONIST into the exam room. Indicates stool.)* You may have a seat.

DYLAN: *(Sits.)* Thank you.

RECEPTIONIST: Are you wearing contacts?

DYLAN: No! Never!

RECEPTIONIST: *(Gives him a strange look.)* Do you wear glasses?

DYLAN: On this face? Are you kidding me?

RECEPTIONIST: Have you ever had an eye exam before?

DYLAN: No, my mom is... shall we say... controlling.

RECEPTIONIST: Moms usually know when their kids aren't seeing well and need a vision check.

DYLAN: She's a worrywart.

RECEPTIONIST: A worrywart?

DYLAN: And a fun-killer. Everything's going just fine then— bam!— "I made you an appointment to get your eyes checked." I'm like, "Mom, my eyes are fine!" But she doesn't believe me.

RECEPTIONIST: Well, the doctor can ease her fears and determine if we have an issue here.

DYLAN: Oh, there's no issue here. I know for a fact that I don't need glasses.

RECEPTIONIST: Well, let's hope not, then. The doctor will be right in.

DYLAN: Thank you. *(The RECEPTIONIST returns to the desk. DYLAN looks out over the audience and squints as he tries to read the eye chart.)* Good thing I memorized it.

DOCTOR: *(ENTERS RIGHT.)* Good afternoon, Dylan.

DYLAN: Hi! Look, I'm sorry to waste your time, but my mother made me come here today. You know how mothers can be, worrying about everything. About nothing.

DOCTOR: Well, let's just take a look to make sure. *(Takes out a pen flashlight and shines it in each of DYLAN'S eyes.)* Good. Good.

DYLAN: *(Jumps up.)* Told you! *(Starts to the door.)* Okay, see you later.

DOCTOR: Whoa! Wait a minute. We still need to do a few more things here.

DYLAN: Oh! Oh, yeah! The eye chart! *(Turns, but not in the direction of the chart and quickly recites.)* Last line is P-E-Z-O-L-C-F-T-I!

DOCTOR: Wow! I'm impressed. And you weren't even looking at the chart. *(Points out over the audience.)* It's over there. Try that again.

DYLAN: Oh, okay. *(Turns toward the eye chart.)* Last line is: P-E-Z-O-L-C-F-T-I. *(Smiles.)* How was that?

DOCTOR: Dylan, please sit down.

DYLAN: *(Sits down.)* Are you going to write me an all clear? Vision is twenty-twenty!

DOCTOR: Now read me the letter on the first line.

DYLAN: *(Squints.)* E.

DOCTOR: Okay. Now read the second line.

DYLAN: *(Squints.)* P-F-Z-T.

DOCTOR: No. That wasn't even close.

DYLAN: Oh, silly me. I must be nervous. *(Laughs.)* Doctor's make me nervous.

DOCTOR: You want to try it again?

DYLAN: Yes, I do.

DOCTOR: Okay, read the second line again.

DYLAN: *(Speaks so fast it's unintelligible.)* A-B-C-D-E-F—

DOCTOR: Could you say that a bit slower?

DYLAN: *(Soft.)* A-B-C-D-E-F—

DOCTOR: You're reciting the alphabet?

DYLAN: I'm sorry. I'm just…

DOCTOR: Nervous?

DYLAN: Yes! Yes, I am nervous.

DOCTOR: One more try?

DYLAN: Yes, please.

DOCTOR: Okay, read any line to me, then.

DYLAN: *(Thinks. As he speaks, he taps his fingers as if typing.)* A-S-D-F… J-K-L-semi-colon.

DOCTOR: J-K-L-semi-colon? From a keyboard?

DYLAN: *(Jumps up.)* What can I say? *(Shakes the DOCTOR'S hand.)* Thanks for the test! See you later!

DOCTOR: Stop!

DYLAN: *(Stops and turns around slowly.)* I passed, right?

DOCTOR: Dylan, you need glasses.

DYLAN: No, wait! Listen, to me! I get nervous when I'm around doctors. Give me one more chance. Please!

DOCTOR: Are you serious?

DYLAN: Before I was, uh… playing around. I'm ready now. Really ready!

DOCTOR: Okay, go ahead.

DYLAN: *(Squints, then takes a step closer to the eye chart. He takes another step, then another and another, until he is standing on the apron.)* E! That's the top letter. Then F-P. Second line. Then T-O-Z. *(Turns to the DOCTOR and smiles.)*

DOCTOR: Perfect.

DYLAN: See! I told you my eyesight was perfect!

DOCTOR: Now step back here and do it again.

DYLAN: *(Steps back and squints. Defeated.)* I can't.

DOCTOR: Just as I thought. Now have a seat again and let's figure out what strength lens you'll need.

DYLAN: But, you're not listening to me! I don't need glasses.

DOCTOR: Are you driving yet?

DYLAN: No, but I will be next year.

DOCTOR: Well, you can't drive without being able to see.

DYLAN: Oh, yeah. Well, you do have a point.

DOCTOR: *(Picks up a pair of glasses from the desk.)* And look at these fashionable gems right here. These are the latest. Garrett Leight designer glasses. Yes, they are a little on the high end, but if you want a stylish look… *(Looks at his phone.)* I'm sorry. Please excuse me just for a moment. *(Hands DYLAN the glasses.)*

DYLAN: No problem. *(Looks critically at the glasses while DOCTOR reads and responds to a text message.)*

ALEX: *(Goes to the RECEPTIONIST.)* Excuse me. Would it be all right if I checked on my friend?

RECEPTIONIST: Of course you can. He did seem nervous about his exam, so maybe a friend in the room will help calm his nerves. *(Stands.)* Let me show you the way.

ALEX: Thank you. *(Follows RECEPTIONIST to the exam room.)*

DOCTOR: *(Puts the phone down and takes the glasses from DYLAN.)* Coincidentally, these should be near the right strength that you will need, so let's check them out. *(Puts the glasses on DYLAN, then hands him a mirror.)*

DYLAN: *(Looks closely in the mirror.)* Uh…I don't know.

ALEX: I knew it! I knew you needed glasses!

RECEPTIONIST: Wow! Those look great on you!

ALEX: You know, she's right. You almost had me convinced that you'd look like a nerd in glasses, but, wow... *(Shakes his head.)* Wow! You look great, Dylan!

DYLAN: I do?

RECEPTIONIST: It's a really good look on you.

DYLAN: *(Looks in the mirror again, then suddenly.)* Wow! I do look good!

DOCTOR: Try reading the chart now, Dylan.

DYLAN: Last line is O-K-D-V-C!

DOCTOR: Perfect!

DYLAN: I'm able to see! Doctor?

DOCTOR: Yes?

DYLAN: I'm practically blind, you know!

DOCTOR: *(Laughs.)* I know. But not anymore.

ALEX: Way to go, Dylan. You can see now.

RECEPTIONIST: And you look good.

DYLAN: *(Looks in the mirror.)* Hot! I look hot! *(Stands with confidence and struts across the room.)* Look out, world! Here I come! *(ALEX, DOCTOR, and RECEPTIONIST laugh. LIGHTS FADE to BLACK.)*

PHONE-FREE ZONE

CAST OF CHARACTERS

HOST/HOSTESS (E) .... annoyed by the status quo
WAITER/WAITRESS (E) .... craves human interaction
CUSTOMERS (12+) .... always on their phones

SETTING
An Italian restaurant.

PROPERTIES
Five tables with chairs, podium with microphone and menus.
Phones, two glasses of water.

LIGHTS UP on four tables of CUSTOMERS in a restaurant.
ALL are staring at their phones. A HOST stands at a podium
DOWN RIGHT. Two CUSTOMERS ENTER RIGHT, also
staring at their phones.

HOST: *(Greets them.)* *Buona sera!* Welcome! Right this way
and I'll show you to your table. *(Leads them to an empty
table. They continue staring down at their phones as they
follow the HOST.)* Here you go. *(Places menus in front of
them, but CUSTOMERS ignore them.)* Our special today is
porcini ravioli. And it looks like you've already discovered
that we now offer you the option of placing your order
online using our friendly little app. Your waiter will be right
with you. *(Returns to podium.)*

WAITER: *(ENTERS with two glasses of water and sets them
on the table. The CUSTOMERS barely look up from their
phones.)* Good evening. I'll be your waiter this evening,
and I'll be right back to take your order, unless, that is, you
prefer to use our friendly little app. *(Silence.)* Okay. Let me
know if you need anything. *(Crosses to the HOST.)* That
"friendly little app" is cutting into my tips. So far tonight,
everyone has ordered online.

HOST: Which makes you less human—less needed and less appreciated.

WAITER: Tell me about it.

HOST: Look at them. Does anyone have face-to-face conversations anymore?

WAITER: No.

HOST: Do you think they're sitting at the same table but talking to each other through text?

WAITER: Probably. And in between messages, they're on Facebook, checking in, tagging their dinner date—who they're not speaking to—making status updates, jumping over to Twitter, looking at Instagram, reading emails, and googling "what is Jell-O."

HOST: Googling "what is Jell-O"?

WAITER: Yeah. I once read an article about the most googled questions. What is Jell-O? Why did the chicken cross the road? Do jellyfish have brains? Why are people so stupid? What is the meaning of life?

HOST: Deep. Do you think they're finding the meaning of life while staring at their phones?

WAITER: I doubt it. *(Looks at his phone.)* Uh-huh. Table number five just ordered using the app. So much for taking their order. Or getting a decent tip.

HOST: Maybe you could try something different.

WAITER: What?

HOST: Tell them the app is down and you need to take their order.

WAITER: Hey, that's not a bad idea! I'm ready to show the customers my fun and charming personality.

HOST: Go for it. Your livelihood is at stake here.

WAITER: *(Crosses to the new CUSTOMERS.)* People, people, people, it is your lucky day! How might you ask? Well, for starters, our friendly little app is not feeling the love and has crashed. Which means... are you ready for this? Which means, you have the sheer pleasure of letting me be of service to you this fine, fine evening. So! If our host did not tell you, today's special is porcini ravioli. Porcini mushroom and ricotta cheese-stuffed ravioli in a cream sauce. *(Throws an Italian finger-kiss.)* Mmm! So, would you like to start out this evening with an appetizer? Shrimp cocktail? Fried mozzarella sticks? Calamari? Or how about my favorite, cheesy garlic bread? Yummy! *(Pause. The CUSTOMERS don't even glance up.)* Okay, so I'll let you look at the online menu for a moment longer, then return for your order. *(Crosses to HOST.)*

HOST: *(Looks at his phone.)* They just ordered online.

WAITER: What?! But I told them the app is down!

HOST: They got a confirmation that their order was received.

WAITER: What's wrong with these people? They never once even looked at me.

HOST: I know. I see that all the time. No pun intended.

WAITER: I did not take this job to be ignored!

HOST: *(Looks at his phone.)* Their order will be ready in twelve—no, make that eleven—minutes. And when you serve them, don't expect an acknowledgement or a thank you, because they'll be too engrossed in their phones to—

WAITER: I can't take this anymore! People need to wake up, get their heads out of their phones, and make eye contact with each other!

HOST: But they won't. They like their phones too much. Addicted to them like a drug. They can't look away. I don't even think they know what a real conversation is these days.

WAITER: Which means... I need to help them!

HOST: How?

WAITER: See table five over there? They are not getting their food until they give me their order.

HOST: But—

WAITER: No! Let's try this again.

HOST: Good luck.

WAITER: *(Crosses to a different table.)* Would you believe it? The app is down. No orders received, even if you got a confirmation already. I know! Frustrating! Hit me if you want to! *(Silence.)* Go ahead. Hit me. *(Silence.)* Of course I'm teasing, but doesn't that just drive you crazy? To the point you actually have to engage? You know, do things the old-fashioned way? Like... gosh, you know... talk! *(Laughs.)* I know, I know, we love our phones. *(Pulls out his.)* I love mine too, but at some point, yes, at some point you just must put the dumb thing down and talk to people. I know, what a concept, huh? *(Silence.)* So… if you're ready to order, I'm ready to take your order. *(Silence.)* Need another minute? *(Silence.)* Well, okay… *(Hums the Jeopardy tune.)*

HOST: *(Approaches the table. Whispers to WAITER.)* They just re-ordered online.

WAITER: *(Loudly.)* But our app is down!

HOST: Uh… I think it's back up.

WAITER: No, it's not! I need to take their order! *(To the CUSTOMERS.)* And I'm one of those waiters who doesn't need to write down your order. Call it good memorizations skills. Like my good people skills. So, go ahead. I'm ready. *(Silence.)* Okay. Need another minute to look over the menu? *(Silence.)*

HOST: *(Pulls WAITER away from the table.)* Come on, come on. People don't talk these days. They don't need to. Or want to. Or have to.

WAITER: Well, how can you have a relationship without ever talking?

HOST: Texting, I guess. Twitter. Snapchat. And private messages, if you have more to say.

WAITER: This is so wrong! I'll be back. *(Crosses back to the same table.)* Hey, how about a little pic with your waiter for Facebook? You can check in and show the world what fun you are having. *(Silence.)* Or not. Fine! *(Crosses to HOST.)*

HOST: *(Looks at his phone.)* Wow. Look at this. They just gave the restaurant a one-star rating.

WAITER: What? They haven't even tried our food yet!

HOST: They said, "Service is terrible. Don't go there."

WAITER: Service is terrible?! I'm trying to do my job! They're the ones who won't cooperate!

HOST: I know.

WAITER: Well, I'm going to try someone else. Maybe those people are just in a bad mood or something. *(Crosses to another table.)* How is everything? Need anything else? *(Silence.)* Was the food to your satisfaction? *(Silence.)* Okay, well, be sure to take our online survey if you'd like a chance to win a free meal. *(Silence.)* Well, okay then.

(Crosses to another table. Claps his hands loudly.) Was that not the best meal ever? Hello? Did it satisfy your palate? Hello? Earth to customers! *(Silence. Crosses to another table and drums on it.)* Let me tell you, there's nothing like good Italian food, is there? Didn't you just love that cheesy garlic bread? My favorite! *(Silence. Drums on the table again.)* Did I tell you that the cheesy garlic bread is my favorite? *(Silence.)* Would you like a take-home box for the leftovers? *(Silence.)* Yes? No? *(Silence. He crosses back to a previous table and throws his body across it.)* Dessert? Would you like dessert? *(Silence.)* Yes? No? Maybe? *(Silence.)* Oh! Do you want to know what we have for dessert? Amaretto cheesecake. Crème brûlée. Our famous chocolate molten lava cake. Hello? Dessert anyone? Hello? *(Throws his arms in the air and kicks his feet.)* Hello?!

HOST: *(Drags WAITER off the table.)* Come on, come on!

WAITER: Why did you do that? I was about to take their dessert order.

HOST: They ordered online. A tiramisu and an epic chocolate brownie.

WAITER: Well, let me tell you something! They're not getting their dessert until they tell me in person!

HOST: That's not how we do it around here. We don't punish the customers.

WAITER: Oh? Well, I say no dessert until I take your order! *(To HOST.)* I'll be back. *(Returns to the previous table.)* The online app is down. Sorry. So, what will you have for dessert? Amaretto cheesecake? Crème brûlée? *(Silence.)* Did you hear me? The online app is down so you will have to speak to me. *(Silence.)* Speak! Speak!

HOST: *(Pulls him away.)* Stop! They aren't dogs.

WAITER: They might as well be! Look at these people! Can't they see they're prisoners to their phones? They're missing out on real life.

HOST: They like it this way.

WAITER: This calls for drastic measures!

HOST: What are you going to do now?

WAITER: *(Grabs the podium microphone and turns it on.)* Hello? Hello? Anyone out there? I have an announcement to make. Listen up! Listen up, people! This is a phone-free zone, which means you must immediately put away your phones. *(Laughs.)* Yes, that means you must start talking to one another. I know. Awkward! But give it a try. Hey, you might like it. *(Silence.)* Look, I've had it with you people! Put those phones down and try talking to each other for a change! *(Silence.)* Okay, question. How many of you are here on a first date? *(One couple raises their hands.)* Well, good! Good! Now, wouldn't it be exciting to hear each other's voices for the first time? Come on! Come on! Look into each other's eyes and say hello. You can do it!

COUPLE: *(Awkwardly lower their phones and look at each other.)* Hello. *(They smile.)*

WAITER: Well, would you look at that! That's remarkable! *(ALL look to the COUPLE.)* And there you have it. That, my folks, is called communication! So, come on! Put those phones down and talk to one another! Come on! You can do it! *(Suddenly, ALL CUSTOMERS put their phones down and begin talking and laughing.)*

HOST: Wow. I must hand it to you, no one has ever done that before.

CUSTOMER: *(Raises hand.)* Can we order dessert over here?

WAITER: Whoa! Look, I have a customer! A real customer! *(Rushes over, but stops to speak to another table that is waving him down.)* And I'll be with you guys in a minute. I need to take their order first. *(Two new CUSTOMERS ENTER, looking at their phones.)*

HOST: Sorry, but this is a phone-free zone. Do you mind?

CUSTOMER: *(Looks up.)* Oh, sorry. We didn't know. *(Puts phone in pocket.)*

HOST: No problem. It's just that we encourage our customers to enjoy conversations here.

CUSTOMER: Oh, sure. Thanks. *(LIGHTS FADE to BLACK.)*

THE FORT

CAST OF CHARACTERS

TAYLOR (F) .... teenager
ISABEL (F) .... her older sister
MOM (F) .... their mother
NANA (F) .... their grandmother

SETTING
A living room.

PROPERTIES
Coffee table, newspaper, chairs covered in blankets to create a fort. Book, stuffed animals, shopping bags.

LIGHTS UP on a blanket fort in the living room with ISABEL sitting inside. TAYLOR ENTERS, reading a book. She slowly walks past the fort, then suddenly stops, looks up, and turns around.

TAYLOR: What the heck? What are you doing in there?

ISABEL: Sitting.

TAYLOR: But... why?

ISABEL: *(Shrugs.)* I'm trying to find the meaning of life.

TAYLOR: Oh. Did you find it?

ISABEL: No. Not yet. But I'm working on it.

TAYLOR: Well, if you find it...

ISABEL: Hey, remember when we were kids, and we'd build a fort and play inside of it?

TAYLOR: Yeah, like when we were five or six years old. Seriously, what's going on, Isabel? Are you hiding from Mom?

ISABEL: No. Mom's out shopping with Nana. I told you, I'm trying to find the meaning of life.

TAYLOR: In a kid's fort?

ISABEL: Yes. *(TAYLOR crawls into the fort and sits beside her. She quietly stares ahead for a bit, but then looks around.)*

TAYLOR: Something's missing.

ISABEL: What?

TAYLOR: Our stuffed animals.

ISABEL: Think we need them?

TAYLOR: Of course, we need them! What's a fort without stuffed animals?

ISABEL: Maybe you should go grab a few, then.

TAYLOR: Okay. *(Runs OFF and quickly returns with an armful of stuffed animals. She drops them in and climbs back in the fort.)* Got them.

ISABEL: *(Peers out.)* Are there any bad guys out there?

TAYLOR: Of course there are. They're always out there.

ISABEL: At least our fort is surrounded by water.

TAYLOR: And there are alligators in the water.

ISABEL: Thank goodness. So we should be safe.

TAYLOR: Yes. *(Conspires.)* What are we really hiding from? It's Mom, right? You did something bad, right?

ISABEL: Maybe.

TAYLOR: I knew it! Tell me!

ISABEL: It's bad.

TAYLOR: Oh, my gosh! How bad?

ISABEL: Very bad.

TAYLOR: You skipped school and got caught? And Mom's going to get a phone call tonight?

ISABEL: No.

TAYLOR: You forgot to feed Jasper again, and he died from starvation. Oh, Jasper! I'm going to miss him. He was a good dog.

ISABEL: No! Jasper's in the backyard. And don't worry, I fed him.

TAYLOR: Oh, good. *(Thinks.)* I know! You went somewhere you weren't supposed to go. Like to the Grays' house. The twins are always trying to talk you into doing something dumb, like eating a ghost pepper and making a video to post on social media. Did you go to the Grays' house and post something online? And now it's only a matter of time...?

ISABEL: No! No! I didn't go over there.

TAYLOR: Then tell me! Your little sister needs to know!

ISABEL: *(Shakes her head.)* It's bad.

TAYLOR: Tell me, Isabel! I want to know! And I'll help you with whatever it is!

ISABEL: Oh, you can't help me with this.

TAYLOR: Come on. Give me a try.

ISABEL: *(Hesitates.)* Remember how Mom is always saying that if I wreck her car it's the end of me?

TAYLOR: You didn't?!

ISABEL: I did. Big dent in the back bumper. There was this pole, and I didn't see it, and...

TAYLOR: She's going to kill you!

ISABEL: I know!

TAYLOR: Unless she doesn't notice it.

ISABEL: Oh, she'll notice it! It's too big and ugly not to notice.

TAYLOR: Can we hammer it out?

ISABEL: I already tried.

TAYLOR: Blame Jasper?

ISABEL: Blame the dog? I would if I could.

TAYLOR: So Mom hasn't seen it yet?

ISABEL: No, but as soon as she gets home from shopping with Nana, it's all over for me. *(Hugs a stuffed animal.)* Taylor, I want to be six years old again.

TAYLOR: *(Hugs another stuffed animal.)* You know, I might join you. I'll be five years old. Just like the good old days. *(Both stare silently ahead.)* My day isn't going so great either.

ISABEL: What happened?

TAYLOR: I flunked my math test, which means Mom will make me go to tutoring from now on. She keeps warning me that one more bad grade in math, and I'm toast.

ISABEL: I'm sorry, Taylor.

TAYLOR: Math is so confusing. Rational numbers. Irrational numbers. Whole numbers. Real numbers. Natural numbers. Did I mention variables? Those little letters to represent an unknown number? Oh, my head is spinning!

ISABEL: Math is not my best subject either.

TAYLOR: It hurts my brain. It's like I don't think on that side of my head. Not very well, at least.

ISABEL: Yeah, Mom's going to be furious with both of us. You flunked your test, and I wrecked her car.

TAYLOR: I didn't flunk on purpose.

ISABEL: And I didn't wreck her car on purpose. Yeah, Mom's day is about to go from good to bad, just like ours. Sorry, Mom, but I wrecked your car.

TAYLOR: Sorry, Mom, but I flunked my test. *(Both stare ahead.)*

ISABEL: Do you want to play?

TAYLOR: Sure.

ISABEL: Okay, so the bad guys are out there, and we must protect our friends... *(Indicates the stuffed animals.)* ...and ourselves.

TAYLOR: Hopefully there aren't zombies out there, because they could probably cross that moat.

ISABEL: Hopefully the alligators will eat them alive.

TAYLOR: But that's the point. They aren't alive!

ISABEL: Good point. Well, we better get ready. I'll be on the lookout, while you get our ammunition ready. We need lots, just in case.

TAYLOR: *(Grabs the newspaper off the coffee table and starts crumbling it into balls.)* These can be rocks to throw at the bad guys if they try to enter our fort.

ISABEL: Good! Make lots of them. We have to protect ourselves!

TAYLOR: Yeah! We don't want to die. Do we have food?

ISABEL: Sure. Crackers and juice. Just like we had when we were kids.

TAYLOR: I liked crackers and juice.

ISABEL: Me too. We survived for hours on crackers and juice. *(Beat.)* Did you hear that?

TAYLOR: What?

ISABEL: I heard something.

TAYLOR: *(Quickly makes more paper balls.)* The zombies are coming!

ISABEL: I think it's Mom and Nana.

TAYLOR: Here! Take some ammunition! You're going to need it!

ISABEL: I hear them! They're coming! The bad guys are coming!

TAYLOR: I'm scared!

ISABEL: Me too! *(MOM and NANA ENTER, carrying shopping bags. They stop short when they see the fort.)*

MOM: Hey, what's going on?

NANA: Oh, look! They're playing in a fort like they did when they were kids. *(ISABEL and TAYLOR throw the paper balls at MOM. NANA laughs.)* Look out!

MOM: *(Laughs.)* Oh! They're getting me! I think they're trying to destroy me!

NANA: You must be the bad guy.

MOM: *(Laughs, decides to play along, and growls.)* I'm going to get you! *(ISABEL and TAYLOR scream.)*

NANA: Silly girls.

MOM: Okay, girls, enough silliness for the day. Isabel, do you want to drive me to the Quick Mart so I can buy some milk? You need all the driving experience you can get. And Taylor, don't you need to show me your math folder? I want to see how you did on today's test.

ISABEL/TAYLOR: *(Run out of the fort and into NANA'S arms.)* Nana, save us! Please save us!

NANA: *(Laughs.)* I guess I'm one of the good guys. *(Puts her arms around them.)* Of course, I will save you! Grandma will save her girls from anything. So, tell me, who am I saving you from?

ISABEL/TAYLOR: *(Points to MOM.)* Her! *(LIGHTS FADE to BLACK.)*

FOREVER HAS NOW ARRIVED

CAST OF CHARACTERS

ANGEL (E)..Kevin's angel
KEVIN (M)................................. recently-deceased young man
CHARLOTTE (F)... his girlfriend

SETTING
Outside the Pearly Gates.

PROPERTIES
Pearly gates. Glass of water.

LIGHTS UP on ANGEL, standing before the Pearly Gates. KEVIN ENTERS and approaches.

ANGEL: *(Extends his arms.)* Welcome.

KEVIN: *(Looks around, confused.)* Thank you, but… where am I?

ANGEL: Your eternal home.

KEVIN: My what? Eternal home?

ANGEL: Some people call it The Great Unknown.

KEVIN: The great what?

ANGEL: Others call it The Promised Land. I prefer Paradise.

KEVIN: What's going on here? What is this place?

ANGEL: Look behind me. What do you see?

KEVIN: I don't know! Some white gates.

ANGEL: Those are the Pearly Gates. The gateway to Heaven.

KEVIN: Heaven? Did you say… heaven? *(ANGEL nods.)* You mean… I'm dead?!

ANGEL: Your life on Earth did in fact expire. And now, you are here. *(Extends his arms.)* Welcome.

KEVIN: I died? Are you freaking kidding me?

ANGEL: I would not kid you. This is your afterlife.

KEVIN: Oh, no! I'm not dead! I'm dreaming! That's what I'm doing. I'm dreaming. *(Slaps himself.)* I need to wake up. This is a bad dream. Wake up! Wake up, you fool!

ANGEL: Would you care to take a tour?

KEVIN: A tour?

ANGEL: Yes. A heavenly tour. Here, you will see colors you have never experienced in your lifetime. Colors that are not permitted on that dreary place you once called home. Magnificent, brilliant colors. Did I mention the streets are paved in gold?

KEVIN: Did I mention I'm not staying? This is a dream. *(Jumps up and down.)* I have to wake up. Wake up! Wake up, you fool! Hey, do you have a glass of water?

ANGEL: Why, certainly, Kevin. Whatever you need.

KEVIN: How do you know my name?

ANGEL: I know everything. *(Offers him a glass of water.)* Here you go.

KEVIN: Throw it in my face.

ANGEL: You don't wish to drink…?

KEVIN: Come on! Throw it in my face! I hope it's cold. The colder, the better.

ANGEL: But…

KEVIN: Give me that! *(Grabs the water and throws it in his face.)*

ANGEL: Why did you do that?

KEVIN: It didn't work. Why are you still here?

ANGEL: *(Extends his arms.)* Welcome.

KEVIN: Oh, my gosh. It must be true. I'm dead!

ANGEL: The people on Earth are saying you passed away, but the truth is, you have arrived. *(Sings.)* "Oh, happy day! Oh, happy day—"

KEVIN: Look, weirdo, I'm not staying!

ANGEL: No? You wish to go to the Lake of Fire? To the fiery pits of Hell?

KEVIN: No! I wish to go to Earth. To my home. Look, Mr.… Mr. Angel, I'm sorry, but I can't stay.

ANGEL: Oh, Kevin, wait until you see your mansion. When you do, you'll be glad you died.

KEVIN: Oh, no, I won't! *(Points at him.)* I'm telling you, there will be no tombstone with my name on it. No rest-in-peace for this fellow! Because I'm leaving!

ANGEL: Why would you want to leave? Kevin, you have arrived in Paradise.

KEVIN: Because I don't want to be in Paradise, that's why! And because I need to get back to Earth. I have some things back there that I need to finish up. Like my life!

ANGEL: What's gone is gone. What's past is past. Your future now awaits you. Forever has now arrived.

KEVIN: Oh, my gosh! Why can't I wake up? This is a nightmare! *(To ANGEL.)* This is a joke, isn't it? Where's the hidden camera? Over there? Behind those gates? *(Waves.)* Hey! Hey, great joke, guys! *(Fake laughs.)* Great joke. You got me. *(To ANGEL.)* Please tell me the truth. It's a joke, right?

ANGEL: In Heaven, there is no deceit, inaccuracy, or dishonesty. Or may I add, jokes. *(Extends his arms.)* Welcome.

KEVIN: *(Slaps his arms down.)* Stop it! Stop welcoming me! I'm not staying! Do you hear me? I'm not staying. Who are you supposed to be, anyway? The welcoming committee?

ANGEL: Kevin, I am your personal angel to assist you in settling into your new forever home.

KEVIN: *(Grabs ANGEL by the robe.)* Look here, Mr. Angel! I'm not staying! So do your thing and zap me back to planet Earth! Or I'll... I'll... I'll make you sorry! That's what I'll do!

ANGEL: Relax, Kevin. Breathe. Look around. Look at all the beauty. Don't you feel the peace engulfing your soul?

KEVIN: No, I don't feel the peace! Do I look like I feel the peace? Oh, why can't I wake up? *(Takes a deep breath and paces.)* Okay, think. Think. Think. *(Turns to ANGEL, in a calm and kind tone.)* I'm sorry. Really... truly... I'm sorry.

ANGEL: Oh, Kevin, all is forgiven.

KEVIN: Thank you. And I do appreciate your hospitality and kindness. You offering to escort me around Heaven and show me all the brilliant colors my eyes have yet to see.

ANGEL: Shall we begin our tour?

KEVIN: *(Drapes his arm over ANGEL'S shoulder.)* Listen, Mr. Angel, I seriously—I mean, seriously—need to get home. Back to planet Earth. I'd love to stay, and I promise to come back at another time, but you see, I have some things I need to take care of first. So if you don't mind, could you just snap your fingers or blink your eyes or say the magic words and send me back home? Please. Pretty please.

ANGEL: *(Hugs him.)* Oh, Kevin, we're so happy that you're here. Soon, there will be shouts of joy and singing. And reunions with loved ones who have passed away before you. And a new body for you... *(Looks at him.)* Yes, a much-needed new body for you.

KEVIN: *(Pushes him away.)* Stop it! Stop it before I kill you!

ANGEL: Kevin, there is no such thing as death here. Or tears. Don't you feel the love?

KEVIN: No! I feel anger. I'm so angry right now, I could spit blood.

ANGEL: You need to calm down. Breathe. Embrace the love.

KEVIN: So, it's true? I'm dead?

ANGEL: Yes, it's true that you died. But now, you shall live forever!

KEVIN: *(Demands.)* How? How did I die?

ANGEL: You don't remember?

KEVIN: No, I don't remember!

ANGEL: Well, that's probably for the best. The past is the past. How it happened does not matter now.

KEVIN: Tell me—Mr. Angel of truth and peace and love and all that crap—tell me... how did I die? I want to know. I deserve to know.

ANGEL: Kevin, your future is here. Forget about the past. Erase it from your memory.

KEVIN: How can I erase it from my memory if I can't remember it? Tell me! How did I bite the dust?

ANGEL: Bite the dust?

KEVIN: Croak! Kick the bucket! In other words, die!

ANGEL: Would you care to visit the waterfalls? The most magnificent, breathtaking sight you will ever see. If you will, follow me through the Pearly Gates, then we'll head down that radiant street of gold...

KEVIN: That's it! That's the last thing I remember. I was on Main Street.

ANGEL: *(Disgusted.)* Oh, that hideous black asphalt. So horrid. So bleak. So black.

KEVIN: I was running after Charlotte. She's my girlfriend. We had just had a fight.

ANGEL: Kevin, I'm sure she's forgiven you.

KEVIN: I don't know if she's forgiven me or not, because I'm here and she's there! Oh, Charlotte! *(Raises hands and looks heavenward.)* Charlotte, I miss you! Please, please forgive me.

ANGEL: Uh... I don't mean to interrupt, but she's down there. We're up here. If I might ask, what did you do?

KEVIN: I didn't know. At least at first. Everything was fine. A normal weekend. TV. Napping. More TV.

ANGEL: You must have done something.

KEVIN: No. Everything was fine. Then Charlotte stepped in front of the TV with her hands on her hips and gave me one of those looks. I was like, "What? What did I do?"

ANGEL: What did you do?

KEVIN: I'm not sure. It was all so confusing. She said so much. I couldn't seem to grasp it all. But I heard... *(Mimics.)* "You ignore me, and you take me for granted!"

ANGEL: I see...

KEVIN: Then she started crying. But I was like, "Baby, this is the last two minutes of the game. Can this not wait?" I motioned for her to scooch over so I could see the TV, but that was a bad move—a very bad move—because then she ran out the door wailing and crying. So, of course, I jumped up and ran after her.

ANGEL: *(Shakes his head.)* Down that black, tar paved road. But here, we have streets of gold. You must really check them out soon.

KEVIN: I called out to her, "Charlotte! Charlotte! Come back! Charlotte, I'm sorry! Stop! Please! Just stop! Charlotte, baby! I love you. Please! Stop!" I was running out of breath. *(Demonstrates.)* I was chasing her for what seemed like forever. Then I hollered, "Charlotte, wait! I have a question to ask you." *(Gasps for air.)* "Just... just one question!"

ANGEL: And?

KEVIN: And then she stopped.

ANGEL: That's good.

KEVIN: I caught up with her and noticed the tears were gone. Now she was glaring at me. *(Harsh.)* "What?" she asked.

So, there I was standing in the middle of the street, cars honking, people cussing and yelling at me to move, and Charlotte glaring at me. But I didn't care. I did it anyway.

ANGEL: Did what?

KEVIN: *(Drops to one knee, looking at ANGEL.)* "Charlotte, will you marry me?"

ANGEL: Oh, my. What did she say?

KEVIN: I don't know. *(Stands.)* The next thing I knew, I'm here.

ANGEL: Yes.

KEVIN: So what happened? How did I get here?

ANGEL: You don't remember?

KEVIN: No.

ANGEL: Flattened like a pancake.

KEVIN: What?

ANGEL: Squished like a spider.

KEVIN: What?

ANGEL: Never saw it coming.

KEVIN: What happened to me? Tell me!

ANGEL: You were run over by a car. *(Extends his arms.)* Welcome.

KEVIN: At the very moment I proposed?

ANGEL: Life is short. You just never know, do you?

KEVIN: But I didn't get to hear her answer. Would she have said yes? I'm sure she would have said yes. We could have spent happily ever after together.

ANGEL: You'll just never know, will you?

KEVIN: Oh, Mr. Angel of truth and love and beauty… *(Under his breath.)* …and all that other crap. Please, if you could just grant me but one wish.

ANGEL: Kevin, I am not a genie. I am an angel of love. *(Smiles.)* And beauty.

KEVIN: But if you could just somehow allow me to go back to Earth and find out what Charlotte's answer would have been before I begin eternity at this place…

ANGEL: All right.

KEVIN: I can?

ANGEL: Yes. I will allow you to go back to Earth for just a moment to hear the answer to your proposal. But only if you understand that you will be flattened like a pancake as soon as she answers you. And then you will return to Paradise.

KEVIN: *(Offers his hand.)* It's a deal. *(ANGEL shakes his hand and steps back. Suddenly, CHARLOTTE APPEARS. He rushes to her.)* Charlotte! Oh, Charlotte!

CHARLOTTE: What?

KEVIN: *(Drops to one knee.)* Charlotte, will marry me?

CHARLOTTE: *(Pause.)* No! *(Stomps OFF. KEVIN grimaces and falls to the ground. After a moment, he stands and turns to ANGEL.)*

ANGEL: *(Extends his arms.)* Welcome.

KEVIN: *(Throws his arms around ANGEL.)* Thank you! Guess it's better to be here than the alternative, huh?

ANGEL: Ready for that tour?

KEVIN: Well, there's one more thing I really need to know.

ANGEL: What's that?

KEVIN: Who won the game? *(LIGHTS FADE to BLACK.)*

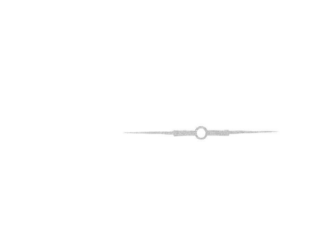

Laurie Allen is a West Texas playwright with eight previously published books of plays and scenes for young adults, including top-selling *Power Plays, Thirty Short Comedy Plays for Teens, Comedy Scenes for Student Actors,* and *Sixty Comedy Duet Scenes.* She got hooked on playwriting when her very first play won a one-act play competition. Since then, her plays have been selected for over forty productions in play festivals worldwide, including "the biggest little play festival in the world" in Sydney, Australia. In addition to her nine books with Meriwether Publishing, Laurie is published by Pioneer Drama Service plus four other publishers. Her plays for teens have enjoyed wide success across the United States, with several of her high school competition pieces succeeding in national competitions. Laurie's works include a wide spectrum of styles from comedy to intense drama and are extremely popular with teens and young adults.